Harvard
Business
Review

ON

CRISIS

MANAGEMENT

THE HARVARD BUSINESS REVIEW PAPERBACK SERIES

The series is designed to bring today's managers and professionals the fundamental information they need to stay competitive in a fast-moving world. From the preeminent thinkers whose work has defined an entire field to the rising stars who will redefine the way we think about business, here are the leading minds and landmark ideas that have established the *Harvard Business Review* as required reading for ambitious businesspeople in organizations around the globe.

Other books in the series:

Harvard Business Review

ON

CRISIS

MANAGEMENT

A HARVARD BUSINESS REVIEW PAPERBACK

The *Harvard Business Review* articles in this collection are available as
individual reprints. Discounts apply to quantity purchases. For information and ordering please contact Customer Service, Harvard Business
School Publishing, Boston, MA 02163. Telephone: (617) 783-7500 or
(800) 988-0886, 8 A.M. to 6 P.M. Eastern Time, Monday through Friday.
Fax: (617) 783-7550, 24 hours a day. E-mail: custserv@hbsp.harvard.edu.

Library of Congress Cataloging-in-Publication Data
Harvard business review on crisis management.
      p.   cm. — Harvard business review paperback series)
      Includes index.
      ISBN 1-57851-235-2 (alk. paper)
      1. Crisis management.   2. Industrial management.   3. Strategic
planning.   I. Harvard business review.   II. Title: Crisis management.
III. Series.
HD49.H37   2000
658.4′056—dc21   99-28481
                                                CIP

*The paper used in this publication meets the requirements of the Ameri-
can National Standard for Permanence of Paper for Publications and
Documents in Libraries and Archives Z39.48-1992.*

Contents

Harvard Business Review

ON

CRISIS

MANAGEMENT

Managing the Crisis You Tried to Prevent

NORMAN R. AUGUSTINE

There is a tide in the affairs of men,
Which, taken at the flood, leads on to fortune;
Omitted, all the voyage of their life
Is bound in shallows and in miseries.
—WILLIAM SHAKESPEARE

Executive Summary

NEWS REPORTS ANNOUNCING that yet another business has stumbled into a crisis—often without warning and through no direct fault of its management—seem as regular as the tide. And the spectrum of business crises is so wide that it is impossible to list each type. On a single day this year, the *Washington Post* reported a series of crashes suffered by American Eagle Airlines, the bankruptcy of Orange County, and Intel's travails with its Pentium microprocessor. Other noteworthy crises have been the *Challenger* space shuttle explosion, the "incident" at the Three Mile Island nuclear reactor, and the series of deaths resulting from cyanide adulteration of Tylenol capsules.

Fortunately, argues Norman Augustine, almost every crisis contains within itself the seeds of success as well as the roots of failure. Finding, cultivating, and harvesting that potential success is the essence of crisis management. And the essence of crisis *mis*management is the propensity to take a bad situation and make it worse. Augustine has distinguished six stages of crisis management and makes recommendations for dealing with each: avoiding the crisis, preparing to manage the crisis, recognizing the crisis, containing the crisis, resolving the crisis, and profiting from the crisis.

Augustine concedes that only the truly brave or the truly foolish would make the claim that one person, sitting atop a corporate hierarchy, can successfully guide the daily actions of thousands of employees. But, he argues, the one aspect of business in which a chief executive's influence is measurable is crisis management. Indeed, the very future of an enterprise often depends on how expertly he or she handles the challenge.

From this incisive passage in *Julius Caesar*, Shakespeare shows himself to be not only a brilliant poet and dramatist but also an excellent businessperson. For as regular as the tide are headlines announcing that yet another business has stumbled into a crisis—often without warning and sometimes through no direct fault of its management. Earlier this year, a single day's copy of the *Washington Post* reported the almost unprecedented series of crashes suffered by American Eagle Airlines; the possible connection between some of the crashes and aircraft built by the French company Avions de Transport Regional; the bankruptcy of Orange County, California, stemming from speculation in leveraged derivatives; and Intel's travails with its Pentium microprocessor. All in all, a good day for bad news. Business as usual, some might say.

The airline, financial securities, and computer industries are, of course, not alone in facing crises. And the tribulations of 1995 are hardly unique. Throughout history, there has been no shortage of business crises. In 1637, speculation in Dutch tulip bulbs peaked at today's equivalent of more than $1,000 per bulb and the market collapsed under its own weight, presenting financially wrenching crises for speculators and their backers. In 1861, the infant Pony Express met its sudden demise when Western Union inaugurated the first transcontinental telegraph.

Almost every crisis contains within itself the seeds of success as well as the roots of failure.

In 1906, the San Francisco earthquake devastated the city and its banking community—except for A.P. Giannini, whose small Bank of America continued making loans during the crisis and went on to become one of the world's largest banks. In 1959, the Food and Drug Administration seized a tiny part of the nation's cranberry crop because it contained a small residue of weed killer, causing the bottom to drop out of the cranberry market right in the midst of the Thanksgiving season. In the 1970s, a number of large insurance companies faced possible bankruptcy as a result of the Equity Funding scandal when they discovered that they had been paying off large sums to nonexistent policyholders. In the past few years, a trusted manufacturer of baby food admitted that its "apple juice" was actually flavored sugar water; syringes inexplicably turned up in the cans of a popular cola brand; and a major oil company's obsolete drilling rig became a rallying point for a radical environmental group.

Almost every crisis contains within itself the seeds of success as well as the roots of failure. Finding, cultivating, and harvesting that potential success is the essence of crisis management. And the essence of crisis *mis*management is the propensity to take a bad situation and make it worse. Many would argue, for example, that President Richard Nixon's cover-up of the Watergate break-in created a bigger crisis than the original transgression alone would have produced.

It is reasonable to ask at this point, What qualifies Norm Augustine to talk about crisis management? Did he take courses in the subject? Does he have an advanced degree in crisis management? Has he published scholarly papers on how to contain crises successfully?

Regrettably, the answer to all those questions is no. No diplomas hang in my office effusively declaring in Latin my expertise in "crisisology." When it comes to crisis management, I am a graduate only of the school of hard knocks. But I have acquired quite a bit of scar tissue over the years as a result of an impeccable sense of timing that has often put me in exactly the wrong place at precisely the right time. Consider that I:

- began my engineering career somewhat inauspiciously by witnessing the first rocket for which I had any responsibility explode ignominiously after a 250-*millisecond* flight—a mere 240,000 miles short of the moon!

- joined the secretary of defense's staff in the Pentagon just as the Vietnam War engulfed the nation;

- joined the mammoth LTV Corporation during the very week in which the founder and CEO, James Ling,

was ousted and bankruptcy suddenly loomed on
the horizon;

- rejoined the government as a presidential appointee
  just in time to witness the resignation of the president
  of the United States;

- was confirmed as assistant secretary of the army just
  one month before a war erupted in the Middle East
  and right before the government of South Vietnam
  collapsed;

- served as under secretary of the army during a variety
  of crises such as the "tree cutting" confrontation in
  the Korean demilitarized zone, when some believed
  that the U.S. response would likely trigger World War
  III;

- assumed responsibility for the largest operating unit
  of Martin Marietta just as the corporation was confronted with a hostile takeover attempt;

- joined the board of a major bank just before the
  nation's banking industry imploded;

- joined the board of a major petroleum company just
  before one of its processing facilities *ex*ploded;

- became CEO of the largest defense R&D contractor in
  the nation shortly before the collapse of the Berlin
  Wall and the subsequent free fall of the U.S. defense
  budget;

- assumed the chairmanship of the American Red Cross
  just as a series of once-a-century natural disasters
  struck the nation—including earthquakes, floods,
  fires, and hurricanes—and at a time when military
  conflicts were breaking out all over the world and

unfounded concerns were arising that the nation's blood supply had been contaminated with HIV.

As a result of this flawless sense of timing, I have assembled ample evidence that there is no magical 9-1-1 number you can call to extricate yourself from such predicaments. You get into a fix; you get yourself out of it. It's that simple. There is no way to run the sausage machine backward and get pigs out of the other end. After all, if the solution were easy, it wouldn't be a crisis.

In business as in life, crises come in as many strains as the common cold. The spectrum is so wide that it is impossible to list each type. Product-related crises alone range from sudden outright failures (the collapsed walkways in the newly built Hyatt hotel in Kansas City, Missouri, in 1981) to unanticipated side effects (lung diseases associated with asbestos) to gradual obsolescence (gas lamps, slide rules, citizens band radios, mimeographs, and buggy whips). Some product crises are completely beyond the control of management. Consider the experience of a major brewing company when a bottle of its premium beer purchased in Florida was found to contain a dead mouse. This rodent became more famous than Mickey until it was determined to be uniquely a native of Florida whereas the beer had been bottled in Colorado.

Another category of business crisis results from accidents, such as airplane and train mishaps, that result in loss of life and erode public confidence. These incidents often attract negative publicity out of proportion even to their tragic consequences. For example, it would take two 747 crashes per week to equal the number of people killed on U.S. highways in the same period, but automobile crashes rarely make headlines the way airplane crashes do. One category of accident, which we might call *technologically charged*, involves the failure of advanced technologies that the public had come to believe were foolproof. This category includes the 1967 Apollo spacecraft fire, in which three astronauts died, the 1979 "incident" at the Three Mile Island nuclear reactor, and the 1986 *Challenger* space shuttle tragedy.

In this era of burgeoning technology, crises stemming from engineering failures will continue. I vividly recall, in the agonizing hours after the *Challenger* explosion, poring over the initial flight data when it appeared that Martin Marietta's hardware had caused the failure. As it turned out, our external fuel tank was not the culprit. But the soul-searching we endured was not an experience any of us soon forgot.

There also are crises that arise from labor disputes, such as those confronted by Kohler, International Harvester, Caterpillar, major-league baseball, and the U.S. air-traffic-control system. And there are crises that stem from financial difficulties—a sudden lack of cash—such as those encountered by Chrysler in the 1970s, the savings and loan associations in the 1980s, and a number of department store chains in the 1990s. Finally, there is the mother of all business crises, one that Martin Marietta experienced at close range: the hostile takeover attempt.

In analyzing the gamut of business crises, we can distinguish six stages of crisis management.

Stage 1: Avoiding the Crisis

Next week there can't be any crisis. My schedule is already full.
     —Henry Kissinger while Secretary of State

The first stage, not surprisingly, is prevention. Amazingly, it is usually skipped altogether, even though it is the least costly and the simplest way to control a potential crisis. The problem may be that crises are accepted by many executives as an unavoidable condition of everyday existence.

This chronic carelessness stems from a blind spot common among business executives—and especially chief executive officers: They actually believe that they are in control of their companies' fortunes. The one redeeming virtue of this blind spot is its ultimately positive effect on the executive's humility. Remember when the chairman of New York's Consolidated Edison, Charles Luce, reassuringly announced during a television interview in July 1977, "The Con Ed system is in the best shape in 15 years, and there's no problem about the summer." Three days later, the entire New York metropolitan area was plunged into 24 hours of darkness in the legendary "Blackout of '77."

Perhaps the best place to begin the search for prevention is suggested in one of my newer laws, which I discovered after my book of laws was published: Tornadoes are caused by trailer parks. Although this may at first seem a dubious proposition, there is empirical evidence to back it up.

Survey the landscape continuously for "trailer parks." That is, make a list of everything that could attract troubles to the business, consider the possible consequences, and estimate the cost of prevention. This exercise is, of course, not much fun, which probably explains why relatively few businesspeople carry it out. Obviously, some of the items on the list will prove to be outside a CEO's control—but the *response* to those items is very much within it. Lacking control over the origin of a problem does not exempt you from living with its consequences.

Why do major corporations encounter so many crises? It is useful to point out that General Motors has about the same number of employees as San Francisco has citizens; that AT&T is about the same size as Buffalo, New York; and that Lockheed Martin is the size of Spokane, Washington. Executives must keep in mind that almost any one of thousands of employees can plunge an entire corporation into a crisis through either misdeed or oversight, as the recent collapse of the venerable Barings Bank made abundantly clear. This type of employee is addressed in my Law of the Cross-eyed Discus Thrower: He seldom wins any prizes, but he sure keeps the crowd on its toes.

Discretion and privacy can be critical to avoiding some kinds of crises, such as those that result from leaks during a sensitive negotiation. Although Lockheed Martin and its predecessors have been credited with an uncanny ability to keep plans private when they need to, even these organizations have almost always fallen short of perfection. In the case of Martin Marietta's $3 billion purchase of General Electric Aerospace in 1993, secrecy was maintained for 27 high-pressure days, only to have the news break into the media two hours before the planned announcement. As for Martin Marietta's and Lockheed's negotiations with each other, the companies stayed out of the newspapers for five and a half months but suffered a leak at midnight before the planned 8 a.m. announcement. And even those relative successes were not without their unsettling moments.

For example, during the discussions between GE and Martin Marietta, officials met mostly in a special work area on the fifty-third floor of an office building in Rockefeller Center. Nearly 100 people who came to be known as the "hole in the wall gang" were hidden away there, pursuing the legal, financial, operational, and personnel aspects of the deal—hoping they would not be noticed in the everyday activity of Manhattan. Work continued virtually around the clock, with meals served at all hours right in the work area. You can perhaps imagine the collective chagrin when the chief financial officer of GE walked out of the building into the virtually empty streets of New York at about 3 a.m. only to be greeted by a man who suddenly erupted from a manhole and remarked, "Oh, the meeting up on 53 must be over," and then disappeared into the manhole just as quickly as he had appeared. To this day, his identity is not known.

If you need to maintain secrecy, limit involvement to as few people as possible and certainly only to those whose discretion can be trusted absolutely. Each participant should be required to sign a nondisclosure agreement. Negotiations should be conducted as quickly as is practicable. Finally, as much apparent uncertainty as possible—engineers would say "noise"—should be inserted into the process so that any accurate leak will be drowned in a sea of false leads. Even so, you should expect everything to leak anyway. You will seldom be disappointed.

Managements thus lead highly precarious existences, but they can minimize their organization's exposure to risk by making clear to employees what behavior is expected of them. The challenge is to be clear in our *own* minds what we truly want from employees. We usually cannot seek revenue growth without also expecting increases in expenses; we cannot encourage risk taking and then be surprised if some of the risks result in greater exposure. In the preventive phase, an executive must try to minimize risks and to be certain that those that must be taken are commensurate with the returns expected. The risks that cannot be avoided must be properly hedged. The real problem, however, is that perfect prevention is perfectly unattainable.

Stage 2: Preparing to Manage the Crisis

Today my stockbroker tried to get me to buy some 10-year bonds. I told him, "Young man, at this point I don't even buy green bananas."
    —the late congressman Chet Holifield,
      when he was getting on in years

Most executives, preoccupied with the market pressures of the present quarter, are not inclined to pay much attention to planning for future crises. This brings us to the second stage of crisis management: preparing for that circumstance when prevention doesn't work—that is, making a plan to deal with a variety of undesirable outcomes if disaster does strike. It is instructive here to recall that Noah started building the ark *before* it began to rain.

Steven Fink, a prominent management consultant, wrote in his book *Crisis Management* that everyone in a position of authority "should view and plan for the inevitability of a crisis in much the same way [one] views and plans for the inevitability of death and taxes: not out of weakness or fear, but out of the strength that comes from knowing you are prepared to . . . play the hand that fate deals you." His survey of the *Fortune* 500's CEOs found that senior managers may suffer from a severe lack of crisis preparedness but certainly not from a lack

When preparing for a crisis, it is instructive to recall that Noah started building the ark before *it began to rain.*

of confidence that they can handle a crisis. Eighty-nine percent of those who responded said that crises in business are as inevitable as death and taxes, yet 50% said they did not have a plan for dealing with crises. Nevertheless, fully 97% felt confident that they would respond well if a crisis occurred. These CEOs are generally the sort who hide their own Easter eggs. They remind me of my young son many years ago at the start of his soccer season, who arrived in uniform at the breakfast table to announce, "We're really gonna get 'em this year. Last year, we were too overconfident."

We must make plans for dealing with crises: action plans, communication plans, fire drills, essential relationships. Most airlines have crisis teams at the ready, along with special telecommunications and detailed contingency plans. Almost all companies today have a backup computer system in case a natural disaster or other catastrophe disrupts their primary system. At Lockheed Martin, we maintain at a central location all the supplies we need to communicate in writing with every member of each key constituency group. A letter can arrive at the home of each of 170,000 employees or 45,000 shareholders within two or three days. As it happens, Martin Marietta used this system on a number of occasions.

Elizabeth Dole, president of the American Red Cross—an organization whose very purpose is to deal with crises—points out another important advantage of anticipating and planning for crises. She recently told me, "The midst of a disaster is the poorest possible time to establish new relationships and to introduce ourselves to new organizations. . . . When you have taken the time to build rapport, then you can make a call at 2 A.M. when the river's rising and expect to launch a well-planned, smoothly conducted response."

And practice counts when planning for the unavoidable. In August 1989, a 1,000-member joint federal-state emergency disaster team tested an earthquake-reaction plan in San Francisco. A scant six weeks later, the powerful Loma Prieta earthquake struck the city, collapsing buildings and starting fires. It is likely that many lives were saved as a result of the relatively smooth handling of evacuations and medical emergencies.

One of the darkest moments of my own career occurred because we did not prepare an adequate contingency plan. Martin Marietta was on the verge of closing the General Electric Aerospace deal—a deal that had been put together on a handshake with Jack Welch of GE and that moved forward quickly. In a midnight meeting a few days before the sale was to take place, evidence suddenly appeared that the Justice Department might not approve pivotal elements of the transaction because of alleged antitrust concerns. Had the transaction cratered at that point, it is likely that GE and Martin Marietta stockholders would have lost overnight approximately $2 billion in market value that they had gained when the combination originally was announced. As Casey Stengel once said, "I've had no experience with that sort of thing, and all of it has been bad."

At that midnight hour, Martin Marietta's top two executives—both engineers—learned to their chagrin that the definition of *high probability* is highly subjective. To the dozen or so lawyers from some of the nation's most prestigious—or, at least, most expensive—firms, *high probability* meant considerably more than fifty-fifty, perhaps even a 70% chance of success. To the engineers, it meant more like 99% or better.

Thus the leadership of each company suddenly found itself plunged into a predicament that it had considered extremely remote until that moment. Fortunately, we were able to put together the evidence needed to resolve the Justice Department's questions and thereby save the deal. When the merger finally won approval, both companies' executives empathized with Winston Churchill's remark, "Nothing in life is so exhilarating as to be shot at without result."

In preparing for crises, it pays to search for subtleties—the second-order effects. I once asked the legendary aviator General Jimmy Doolittle to name the greatest hazard that pilots faced in the pioneering days of aviation. His answer was unexpected but no doubt accurate. "Starvation," he replied. Drills like the one in San Francisco help identify these second-order effects because the devil *is* in the details and the cost of overlooking them can be high. For example, in the aftermath of Hurricane Andrew in 1992, the telephone companies discovered that one of the principal shortages in southern Florida was not poles, wires, or switches but day care centers. Many of the phone companies' field-operations employees had children and relied on day care. When the centers were destroyed by the hurricane, someone had to stay home to take care of the children—thereby reducing the workforce at the moment when it was needed the most. The problem eventually was solved by soliciting retirees to tend ad hoc day care centers, thereby freeing working parents to assist in restoring the telephone network.

Experience suggests a number of useful preparations for dealing with an upheaval: establishing a crisis center, making contingency plans, selecting in advance the members of the crisis team, providing ready and redundant communications, and—most important—testing those communications. As the United States government has learned in circumstances ranging from the attack on Pearl Harbor to the capture of the *Pueblo* by North Korea, the best-laid plans are worthless if they cannot be communicated.

Stage 3: Recognizing the Crisis

If you can keep your head when all about you are losing theirs, it's just possible you haven't grasped the situation.
—humorist Jean Kerr

This stage of crisis management is often the most challenging: recognizing that, in fact, there is a crisis. Executives who refuse to face reality should be mindful of the bright if inexperienced chemistry student who warned, "When you smell an odorless gas, it's probably carbon monoxide." In general, you need to understand how others will perceive an issue and to challenge your own assumptions.

Companies sometimes misclassify a problem, focusing on the technical aspects and ignoring issues of perception. But it is often the public perception that causes the crisis. In the case of Intel Corporation's tribulations with its Pentium microprocessor in late 1994, the college professor who first discovered that the chip had trouble performing complex mathematical calculations precisely contacted Intel to report the anomaly he had observed. So confident was the company in its product that it reportedly gave the professor a polite brush-off. Turning to the Internet to see if others could confirm the problem he had encountered, he

Companies sometimes misclassify a problem, focusing on the technical aspects and ignoring issues of perception.

triggered an avalanche of some 10,000 messages, including such scathing jokes as "Why didn't Intel call the Pentium the 586? Answer: Because they added 486 and 100 on the first Pentium and got 585.999983605."

The root cause of the crisis was that Intel had reacted to a technical problem when it really had a public relations problem. The ensuing media coverage was devastating, featuring such headlines as "Intel . . . the Exxon of the Chip Industry," "Firm Reverses Itself on Pentium Policy," "Humble Pie," and "Intel to Replace Its Pentium Chips." CEO Andrew Grove later said, "To some people, [our policy] seemed arrogant and uncaring. We apologize for that." Shortly thereafter, the company was reported to have taken a $475 million charge against earnings. Meanwhile, the millions of Internet users had been treated to such derisive jokes as "It's close enough. We say so" and "You don't need to know what's inside." Ironically, once the company did offer to replace the chip, few users accepted. Only an estimated 1% to 3% of individual consumers (who constitute two-thirds of the purchasers of computers with Pentium chips) took up the offer. It wasn't that people wanted a new chip; it was just that they wanted to know that they could get a new chip if they wanted one. As everyone knows, banks don't want borrowers to pay off their loans; they just want to know that borrowers *can* pay off their loans.

The problem in this stage of crisis management is that perception truly does become reality. We saw this principle at work last summer in the seemingly straightforward plan of Royal Dutch/Shell Group to dispose of the Brent Star oil-storage rig by sinking it in a deep area of the Atlantic Ocean. Despite the approval of the relevant governments and the blessing of many environmentalists, the plan was suddenly thrown into disarray when

Greenpeace protesters attempted to land a helicopter on the oil rig's deck. The company responded by trying to keep the helicopter away with water cannons. As the *Wall Street Journal* reported the controversy, "Shell had made a strategic error. In a world of sound bites . . . one image was left with many viewers: A huge multinational oil company was mustering all its might to bully what was portrayed as a brave but determined band." Whatever the reality of the situation, Shell found its plan foundering on the shoals of worldwide media perception.

A variation on this theme is a syndrome that I call *crisis creep.* We experienced it at Martin Marietta last year in a particularly embarrassing incident. We were castigated by a media outlet that accused one of our major plants of charging the government for the cost of a Smokey Robinson concert for its employees. That's not how the company would have characterized the situation, but it's pretty much the way it was coming across in the local media. Soon the national media began to pick up the story, and several members of Congress threatened to hold hearings.

As the situation was explained to me, our company's employees voluntarily contribute some 10 million hours of unpaid overtime each year, a donation that primarily benefits customers—in this case, the government. As a token of appreciation, the company had over many years developed the custom of occasionally doing something special for employees: giving their children tickets to the Shriners' Circus, holding a family picnic, or taking groups to see the local baseball team in action. Company accountants had assured management that the practice of including such events in the cost of products was altogether legal, fully disclosed, and fairly common as a commercial practice. Further, it constituted only about one

one-hundredth of 1% of the cost of the products being sold—an amount greatly offset by the overtime the employees contribute.

As the explanations continued, I couldn't help but think of Groucho Marx's penetrating question "Are you going to believe what you see or what I'm telling you?" A reasonable question to ask my earnest colleagues was, If we are so thoroughly in the right, why is it that in a city with a population of more than 1 million we can't find one person who doesn't think we are dead wrong? Somehow, without realizing it, the company had crossed the threshold from family picnics to Smokey Robinson concerts and, in so doing, offended the public's sensibilities. We quickly issued a public apology for our lack of sensitivity, indicated that all the costs incurred would be taken out of the corporation's profits, and promised that we would never again make the same error of judgment. Once those steps had been taken, the drumbeat of criticism ceased almost overnight.

But sometimes even stronger warnings of impending crisis go unheeded. For example, nearly a decade before the Hubble Space Telescope was launched, two different tests conducted by the manufacturer of the telescope's primary mirror indicated that something was wrong with the precision of its surface. Shortly after the launch, the "Trouble with Hubble" began publicly when the spacecraft was discovered to suffer from nearsightedness. The mirror manufacturer's engineers had been so confident in their design that they simply had disregarded the test results. Similarly, before the failure of the *Challenger*, a series of memorandums to the solid rocket motor company's management from various of its engineers contained such impassioned pleas, highly unusual for technical documents, as "HELP! The seal task force is constantly being delayed by every possible means." Another memo implored, "If we do not take immediate action to . . . solve the problem with the field joint . . . we stand in jeopardy of losing a flight along with all the launchpad facilities." As history records, those calls went unheeded. The words of Demosthenes seem to apply: "Nothing is easier than self-deceit. For what each man wishes, that he also believes to be true."

There are, of course, positive examples of management's recognizing crises as they develop and moving effectively to resolve them. Procter & Gamble's response to the early fears that Rely tampons might be causing toxic shock syndrome is such a case. Most observers give high grades to P&G for stopping production and withdrawing the product from the market based on the relatively tenuous but disconcerting evidence becoming available. The management's quick and courageous actions to protect the health of those who use P&G products—and, not incidentally, the company's reputation—

Asking the people responsible for preventing a problem if there is a problem is like delivering lettuce by rabbit.

proved far more important over the long term than the hundreds of millions of dollars that the decision must have cost over the short term. The company avoided long-term damage by putting into practice a principle generally embraced by business executives but all too often overlooked during a crisis: The interests of the customer must come first. Obviously, when it came to their health and safety, P&G's customers' greatest concern was whether they truly could trust the company whose

products they had been using for years. P&G put trust
and open communication with customers above all other
corporate concerns and emerged a long-term winner.

Experience suggests that we listen to people throughout the organization when looking for information about
a crisis. In the words of Bellcore CEO George Heilmeier,
"The natives have the maps." Thus the phrase *We have
had an incident*, when spoken by the head of any operating entity, should be one of the most recognizable alarms
in a CEO's repertoire. Similarly, when an engineer
reports, "We have experienced an anomaly," he or she
usually means that there has been a collision between a
space rocket and a commercial jetliner and the debris
has landed on a nuclear power plant.

In the recognition stage, independent investigators, as
well as insiders, are needed to assist in understanding
the situation. Asking the people who were responsible
for preventing a problem whether or not there is a problem is like delivering lettuce by rabbit. There are, of
course, costs associated with using independent experts,
but, as the old adage goes, if you think an expert is
expensive, try hiring an amateur.

Stage 4: Containing the Crisis

When you come to a fork in the road, take it.
—Yogi Berra

This stage of crisis management requires triage: stopping the hemorrhaging. This is the phase in which the
tough decisions have to be made and made fast. For
example, should the area surrounding the Three Mile
Island nuclear reactor be evacuated, with the almost certain chaos that such an action would entail, or should

people be told to remain where they are and be put at risk? When deaths occurred in Chicago, should Johnson & Johnson promptly recall all Tylenol capsules, at great cost, or wait for more conclusive evidence of a nation-wide threat? In this phase, decisiveness is critical—and the timeless advice of Yogi Berra is sound: *Some* reasonable, decisive action is almost always better than no action at all.

The problem in this stage is that usually you don't know what you don't know. There may be too little information or there may be far too much, with no way to sift out what is important. The report of the Kemeny Commission, which investigated the Three Mile Island "incident," included the following statement: "During the first few minutes of the accident, more than 100 alarms went off, and there was no system for suppressing the unimportant signals so that operators could concentrate on the significant alarms. Information was not presented in a clear and sufficiently understandable form."

Unfortunately, the demand for the CEO to clarify a murky situation might well describe the early phase of most crises. Crisis situations tend to be accompanied by conflicting advice—with the legal department warning, "Tell 'em nothin' and tell 'em slow," the public relations department appealing for an immediate press conference, the shareholder relations department terrified of doing anything, and the engineers all wanting to disappear into their labs for a few years to conduct confirmatory experiments. My experience has been that it is preferable to err on the side of overdisclosure, even at the risk of harming one's legal position. Credibility is far more important than legal positioning.

In the Exxon *Valdez* incident, the lawyers advised against admitting any guilt in order to be better able to defend the company's position. In the end, the company suffered a multibillion-dollar jury verdict *and* a tarnished reputation. Sometimes a CEO must override the lawyers. And the truth is that even in the face of contradictory evidence and confusing advice, one cannot simply remain silent. James Lukaszewski, a specialist in communications, counsels, "Say something. If you aren't prepared to talk . . . reporters will find someone who is." "No comment" is an unacceptable response in today's fast-forward world of telecommunications. So, too, is "We haven't read the complaint" or "A mistake was made." My son tumbled to the concept of detached responsibility at the age of four when he dismissed the question of how shoe polish had gotten all over the living-room wall with a polite "Sometimes that happens."

Perplexed over the issue of how much to say and when, I sought the advice of one of America's greatest businesspeople: Warren Buffett. His advice, as you might expect, was both pragmatic and brilliant.

Companies that have decided what they stand for in advance of a crisis manage the crises best.

"First," he said, "state clearly that you do *not* know all the facts. Then promptly state the facts you *do* know. One's objective should be to get it right, get it quick, get it out, and get it over. You see, your problem won't improve with age." This, needless to say, is exactly how he dealt with the crisis at Salomon Brothers a few years ago.

And what is the principal message you wish to convey? It has been wisely said that the world is not interested in the storms you encountered but in whether you brought the ship in safely. As a senior executive, you must call on your own conscience. You must set aside for a few minutes the voices of trusted advisers and, in as calm and dispassionate a manner as possible, evaluate in *human* terms the real issues and the real messages. By so doing, you at least have the comfort of defending a position that you believe to be correct. As far as I know, Charles Barkley of the Phoenix Suns is the only person who ever got away with claiming that he had been misquoted in his autobiography.

Organizations that have thought through what they stand for well in advance of a crisis are those that manage crises best. When all seems to be crashing down around them, they have principles to fall back on. Johnson & Johnson has said of its highly regarded response to the Tylenol deaths that its actions had been preordained by its widely heralded corporate credo; that is, no other response could even have been contemplated.

Another conclusion from the crises I have studied is the value of immediately dispatching the senior responsible individual to the scene of the problem—usually the CEO. The CEO may know less about the details of the situation than the local management, but his or her physical presence sends two important messages: I care, and I am accountable. The CEO of Union Carbide took this approach during the Bhopal tragedy, when some 2,000 people died as a result of a chemical leak at the company's Indian subsidiary. Although the immediate result was that the CEO found himself in jail, traveling to India had been the proper course. In business, "good" decisions do not necessarily guarantee good outcomes.

One bit of caution about the dispatch-the-CEO theory comes from former secretary of state Lawrence

Eagleburger. "Don't call on the court of last resort until you are at your last resort," he counseled me. For example, if the CEO enters into a union negotiation with the head of the local, the CEO is not likely to be effective with the head of the national union if an impasse arises later. But in situations that truly threaten one's reputation or existence, the CEO belongs in the front lines.

My experiences in the triage stage have taught me four other lessons. First, it is wise to have a dedicated group of individuals working full-time to contain the crisis; others still have a business to operate. That is, a "fire wall" should be built between the crisis management team, led by the CEO, and the business management team, led by an appropriate senior operating person. Too many executives seem to have forgotten the words spoken so generously by Casey Stengel when his New York Yankees won the 1958 World Series: "I couldn'a done it without my players."

Second, a single individual should be identified as the company spokesperson, the one who makes all public comments. This lesson stems from another of my laws: If enough layers of management are superimposed on top of one another, it can be assured that disaster is not left to chance.

Third, a company's own constituencies—its customers, owners, employees, suppliers, and communities—should not be left to ferret out information from the public media. With all the pressures on management to respond to news reporters, one must not neglect those who have a special need for information.

And fourth, a devil's advocate should be part of the crisis management team—someone who can tell the emperor in no uncertain terms when he is wearing no clothes.

Stage 5: Resolving the Crisis

Even if you're on the right track, you'll get run over if you just sit there.
—Will Rogers

In this stage, speed is of the essence. A crisis simply will not wait. It's like wrestling a gorilla: You rest when the gorilla wants to rest. John Lowenstein of the Baltimore Orioles once was asked what could be changed to improve the game of baseball. He answered, "They should move first base back a step to eliminate all the close plays." Unfortunately, it doesn't work that way in baseball or in crises.

Three years ago, the supermarket chain Food Lion suddenly found itself thrust into the public spotlight when it was accused by ABC-TV's *Prime Time Live* of selling spoiled meat. The company's stock plummeted, bottoming out at slightly greater than half its precrisis value. But Food Lion acted quickly, offering public tours of stores, putting large windows in meat-preparation areas, improving lighting, putting workers in new uniforms, expanding employee training, and offering large discounts to draw customers back into stores. The company eventually earned an "excellent" rating from the Food and Drug Administration, and in locations where it had previously been well established, sales soon returned to normal.

Similarly, when accusations were made that the electromagnetic fields generated by cellular telephones caused brain tumors, the manufacturers quickly sought out independent experts who took the facts directly to the public, and the concerns promptly subsided. Pepsi-Cola used a similar approach when syringes were found in cans of its soft drinks. The company promptly and publicly demonstrated that the foreign objects must have been planted by the purchaser. Once again, the furor quickly passed.

Perhaps the most challenging crisis in the history of Martin Marietta occurred in the summer of 1982, when the company suddenly became the target of a hostile takeover attempt by the Bendix Corporation. The laws governing a company's actions in a takeover attempt are complex and impose specific time limits. By striking first and without warning, Bendix achieved an early tactical advantage. However, Martin Marietta, under CEO Tom Pownall's leadership, fought back by issuing a counter-tender offer for the shares of Bendix—a tactic that has become known as the Pac Man defense and that was intended to result in Martin Marietta's gaining effective control of a majority of Bendix's shares, including a large block administered by Bendix's own employee stock-ownership plan. The result was that each company acquired a majority of the other's shares.

In the short space of a month, Martin Marietta alone hired 14 law firms and was litigating in 11 federal district courts, three federal courts of appeals, and three state courts, including the Supreme Court of Delaware. One judge, perplexed by the legal issues involved, invoked the words of Shakespeare, saying to the lawyers of the two parties, "A pox on both your houses!"

The impasse was resolved by intensive negotiation. Allied Corporation, following discussions with Martin Marietta, agreed to step in and merge with Bendix and then swap some of the Martin Marietta stock that Bendix held for the Bendix stock that Martin Marietta held. In the end, Martin Marietta retained its independence.

Stage 6: Profiting from the Crisis

Experience is the name everyone gives to their mistakes.
—Oscar Wilde

The final stage in crisis management is making lemonade from the abundance of available lemons. If a company has handled the previous steps flawlessly (that is, has not somehow managed to make the crisis even worse), the sixth stage offers an opportunity to recoup some losses at least partially and begin to repair the dislocations. One example is the U.S. Army's adroit handling of a highly volatile situation that arose in 1993. Munitions left from the World War I era were found buried in what is now the residential community of Spring Valley in the District of Columbia. A number of homes had to be evacuated, and, understandably, emotions in the community ran high. The army general having overall responsibility in the area personally took charge of the situation, meeting with local citizens in a community forum each evening throughout the crisis. The media always were invited, and questions were answered willingly and candidly. When the crisis had subsided, the local citizenry named a street in their community in the general's honor.

But the canonical example of turning around an emotionally charged crisis is Johnson & Johnson's handling of the Tylenol case. Responding to the series of deaths that resulted from cyanide adulteration of Tylenol capsules, then CEO Jim Burke reasoned that forceful measures were needed to ensure public safety and restore trust in the company's top-selling product. With full-page ads and television spots announcing its intentions, the company pulled 31 *million* capsules from store shelves and home medicine cabinets around the nation, redesigned the packaging, and within three months regained 95% of its precrisis market share. This feat was not accomplished without cost, but the cost of repurchasing a reputation that otherwise would have been severely tarnished would have been infinitely greater.

From a business perspective, the result of the Tylenol crisis was that Johnson & Johnson demonstrated both its concern for its customers and its commitment to the corporation's ethical standards. Although this was a tragic episode, the company clearly was regarded even more highly after the episode than before.

I asked Burke what he would add to this account, and he said he would emphasize two points. First, he cited the axiom that many senior executives seem to overlook: "If you run a public company, you cannot ignore the public." Second, "Institutional trust is a lot more important than most people realize. The operative word is *trust* . . . and whether people will take one's word when one badly needs them to do so will depend on how much confidence has been built in the organization over the years before the crisis occurs."

This is, of course, not particularly good news for U.S. business as a whole. A recent Gallup Poll ranked the American public's confidence in big business at 26%, placing it only slightly ahead of Congress and about equal with newspapers. But, as is often the case, there is a silver lining to be found even in this cloud. When, for example, two spacecraft that had been built by another company failed just after Martin Marietta's purchase of that business, Martin Marietta publicly took full responsibility and voluntarily returned $22 million of profit to the customer. To Martin Marietta's utter surprise, it was given great accolades by the public and the media.

Apparently, expectations for business are so low that a company is given effusive credit simply for doing what is right.

Doing what is right and following the recommendations for each of the six stages, however, do not guarantee the desired outcome. There is one other important ingredient that affects all crisis managers from time to time: luck.

Borrowing once again from Martin Marietta's experiences, bad luck was working for years to develop a new dye for blue jeans that absolutely would not fade. The successful result of this technological tour de force, known as Martin Blue, arrived on the market at precisely the moment when a sudden shift in consumer demand occurred—to prefaded jeans! As John Chalsty, who runs Donaldson, Lufkin & Jenrette, once said of an experience at his own company, presumably with appropriate apologies to Ralph Waldo Emerson, "We had built the perfect mousetrap. Trouble was, that mouse was already dead."

My favorite example of simple, dumb *good* luck relates to the activities of Christopher Boyce, the Russian spy of Cold War infamy and, sadly, the son of a business associate of mine. The young Boyce was then working for TRW in Los Angeles. Or, more accurately, he was working for TRW in somewhat the same way that Premier Nikita Khrushchev must have had in mind when, at the height of the Cold War, he greeted then CIA director Allen Dulles with the remark "You know, you and I have some of the same people working for each other."

Boyce eventually was sentenced to more than 60 years in prison for his actions on behalf of the Soviet Union. While reading *The Falcon and the Snowman*, Robert Lindsey's book chronicling Boyce's escapades, I was stunned to discover that Boyce had solicited a position at Martin Marietta's plant in Denver. At that very moment, I was the general manager in charge of Martin Marietta's plant in Denver! Racing ahead in the text, I learned how executive brilliance had enabled the company to escape this momentous crisis. Boyce, quoted in the book, expressed great chagrin over the fact that he had applied not once but twice for a position at the Denver plant and on both occasions the ever vigilant personnel department had lost his application.

Of course, business executives cannot rely on luck to see them through the crises that inevitably strike at the most inconvenient moments. I know of no board of directors that will contentedly accept as the explanation for major corporate difficulties, "Oh, it was just bad luck." In such instances, I have found, they are likely to agree with legendary baseball manager Branch Rickey that "luck is the residue of design."

In this regard, I have always found compelling the argument of business writer Robert Heller, who said, "The first myth of management is that it exists. The second myth of management is that success equals skill." I came to a similar conclusion in my own book *Augustine's Laws*—a conclusion captured by Law Number 29, which states, "Executives who do not produce successful results hold on to their jobs only about five years. Those who produce effective results hang on about half a decade."

The notion that one person, sitting atop a corporate hierarchy, can regularly and successfully guide the daily actions of tens of thousands of individual employees is a pleasant confection created, some would suggest, by academics and certain business leaders. Only the truly brave or the truly foolish would make this claim. However, the one aspect of business in which a chief executive's influence is measurable is crisis management. Indeed, the very future of an enterprise often depends on how expertly he or she handles the challenge. Crises tend to be highly formative experiences—watershed experiences, sometimes even life-threatening experiences—for a business. Nowhere else is the leadership of a chief executive more apparent or more critical to the long-term prospects of an enterprise.

So by all means avoid involving your business in a crisis. But once you're in one, accept it, manage it, and try to keep your vision focused on the long term. The bottom line of my own experience with crises can be summarized in just seven words: Tell the truth and tell it fast.

Originally published in November–December 1995
Reprint 95602

When an Executive Defects

ANURAG SHARMA AND

IDALENE F. KESNER

Executive Summary

THE NEWS THAT ONE OF THE COMPANY'S senior
managers is leaving comes as a complete surprise to
Paul Simmonds, CEO of Kinsington Textiles, Inc. Ned
Carpenter, KTI's vice president of operations for three
years, writes in his resignation letter that he is leaving for
a better opportunity. Simmonds soon learns that Carpenter's new job is at Daltex, one of KTI's main rivals in the
intensely competitive carpet industry.

Hiring Carpenter had helped Simmonds establish his
reputation as a top-notch manager. Carpenter came to
KTI with lots of ideas and put his enthusiasm to good use.
Three years into a five-year change program, Carpenter
had turned KTI's operations from one of the worst in the
industry to one of the best. He also had helped develop
and plan the upcoming launch of a new fiber coating—
KTI's first breakthrough in years.

In this fictitious case study, Simmonds, along with the company's counsel and vice president of human resources, must figure out how much and what sort of damage control they need. What are they going to tell the company's employees and the media? Should they immediately replace Carpenter with John Brady, the second-in-command of operations? What if Carpenter is taking KTI employees—and strategic information—with him to Daltex? Should Simmonds ask all his managers to sign noncompete agreements—something Carpenter was never asked to do? Should KTI sue Carpenter?

Five experts offer advice about communicating with KTI's employees, the media, and Carpenter himself, and about protecting the company's confidential information.

As PAUL SIMMONDS, CEO of Kinsington Textiles, Inc. (KTI), pulled into the company's parking lot just before dawn, he saw that he wasn't the first one in. Of the two cars already there, the blue Chevy probably belonged to the security guard. But the white Saab belonged to David Murray, the vice president of human resources and a trusted lieutenant.

Simmonds and Murray had stayed at the office late the previous night, discussing how to respond to the sudden resignation of Ned Carpenter, who had been the vice president of operations at KTI for three years. During the evening, Simmonds and Murray had called Rick Craswell, a prominent corporate lawyer on retainer with KTI. The three had decided to meet at Simmonds's office early the next morning.

Life in the Carpet Capital of the World

Although Carpenter's resignation letter said only that
he was leaving for a better opportunity, Simmonds
found out that he was going to work at Daltex, one of
KTI's main rivals in the increasingly competitive carpet
industry. Coming by this information had not been difficult in Dalton, Georgia, where both KTI and Daltex
were located. Dalton was the undisputed carpet capital
of the world. The town's preoccupation with carpets
was evident from the names of local businesses, which
included the Broadloom Breakfast Joint and the Cut-a-
Rug Lounge. More than 250 manufacturing plants were
located in and around the town, and together they
produced about 82% of the more than 1.25 billion
square yards of carpeting made in the United States
each year.

The 25 largest carpet manufacturers accounted for
75% of the industry's production, although the industry
was also populated with many small companies. KTI was
one of the large companies, with $363 million in rev-
enues, market capitalization of approximately $200 mil-
lion, and more than 2,000 employees. Most of KTI's competitors were part of large, diversified conglomerates
with deep pockets to fund a wide array of strategic initiatives. But KTI did not have a parent to fall back on. The
company had to be selective with its investments, priori-
tizing strategic opportunities and investing only in the
areas that seemed to hold the most promise. Furthermore, because KTI was publicly traded—and had been
for 20 years—the company had to consider the stock
market's reaction to significant events.

Industry experts typically described the carpet business as commodity-like and cutthroat. As one executive

put it, "Being in the black or in the red in a given year may be a matter of cost savings on the order of 1 to 2 cents per yard." Despite the intense competition, most of KTI's senior managers believed that there were still some niches where producers could charge a premium for quality, durability, and service.

The company hadn't always been so optimistic. In fact, when Simmonds hired Carpenter away from his post as vice president of operations at a large chemical company in the area, KTI was going through some rough times, a result of outmoded and inefficient manufacturing opera-

Without Carpenter, would KTI lose the ground it had so recently gained?

tions. Simmonds had been CEO for two years at that point, though he had been with the company since graduating from college 20 years before.

Hiring Carpenter helped establish Simmonds's reputation as a top-notch manager. The retiring vice president of operations, who had held the position for 23 years, had long since tired of the job and was more than ready to move to Florida to be near his grandchildren. Carpenter, in contrast, was full of ideas. He came to KTI eager to apply his knowledge of manufacturing in the chemical industry to the carpet industry and to improve the company's production statistics. He even had ideas about producing new types of floor covering to broaden KTI's market. He made good on his enthusiasm. In just three years, Carpenter turned KTI's operations from one of the worst in the industry to one of the best. His departure could prove disastrous for the company's competitive position as well as for the continuity of its internal operations. Carpenter was three years into a five-year change program. Without him, would the program falter? Would KTI lose the ground it had so recently gained?

Too Early to Think Straight

"And what about the new fiber coating?" Murray asked Simmonds, who was staring into his empty coffee cup. "Ned has been working closely with R&D on that for eight months. It's our first real breakthrough in a long time. He knows all about it, and he'll take that knowledge with him."

"We're eighteen months away from a commercial launch," Simmonds said, trying to keep the tenor of the meeting calm.

"But Ned knows all the plans. He *wrote* half of them, for crying out loud," Murray said.

"I know that better than you do," Simmonds said, rubbing his forehead with both hands. "It's too early to think straight."

Craswell raised an eyebrow. "We're going to have to think straight and think fast," he said. "We've been in here for an hour already, and we haven't gotten anywhere. Let's take five minutes to walk around and get some more coffee. Then, Paul, I'd like to hear a little more about how you and Ned worked together."

It was obvious to Murray and to Craswell that Simmonds had been taken by surprise the previous day when he received Carpenter's letter of resignation and that he was especially hurt by the discovery that Carpenter was leaving to work at Daltex. But Murray also knew that some differences had developed between Carpenter and Simmonds.

In particular, the two disagreed about which markets to enter with the company's new coating process. KTI's limited resources prohibited it from hitting the commercial and residential markets simultaneously, especially because those markets did not share distribution channels. Carpenter felt strongly that KTI should go after the highly competitive commercial market as soon as possible, but Simmonds thought that the residential market was a safer first strike. Murray had witnessed several heated conversations between the two men on the issue; who knew how many more they had had in private? Ultimately, they decided to hold off on a decision until they had more information from the R&D department. But Carpenter knew as well as anyone that Simmonds had the final say

"He's privy to strategic information, and we don't know how long he's been negotiating with Daltex."

and that once his mind was made up, as it seemed to be, he wouldn't back down. Murray sympathized with Carpenter on that point. There was some scuttlebutt now and then about Simmonds's tendency to reach decisions too quickly and his difficulty delegating assignments.

There also had been a few sore spots about Carpenter's compensation, Murray recalled. Craswell knew that, too, having been involved in the process of hiring Carpenter three years earlier. But Carpenter's salary was the second highest in the company; how unhappy could he have been?

Simmonds came back from the kitchenette with a refill of his coffee and a chocolate doughnut. "I don't understand why Ned didn't let me know he was unhappy here," he said, not waiting for the other two to sit back down. "If he had indicated that he was dissatisfied, maybe we could have worked something out. I mean, I don't think there was any way I could have seen this coming. There weren't any signs. And what really gets me is that he has been participating in all our meetings. He's privy to strategic information, and we don't know how long he's been negotiating with Daltex."

"Maybe he wasn't unhappy," Murray said. "Maybe Daltex just made him an offer he couldn't refuse. But we can't think about that now. We keep trying to figure out what happened, but that's not what we should be worrying about. We have to decide what kind of damage control we need."

"Well, I think the first thing we need to do is get John Brady in here and offer him Ned's job," Simmonds said slowly. "He's certainly no Ned, but he is the second-in-command in operations, and he's the only person who can continue the change program Ned started without completely running it off the rails."

"I'm not sure we want to move that fast," Murray cautioned. "Suppose Ned is taking some of his people with him? Suppose John Brady is on the list? We need to try to find out how many—if any—people are following Ned out the door."

"Look," Craswell broke in. "I know this isn't my area of expertise, but you need to do *something* fast, before the rumor mill gets going. What are you going to say to your employees? The paper is going to pick up the story by tomorrow at the latest. The local radio and TV stations will have it today."

"But how should we play this?" Simmonds asked. "My guess is that everyone in the company will be as outraged by Ned's move as I am. Can I use this as a rallying cry?"

Murray shook his head. "I think you should play it down," he said. "You don't know what people are really thinking. You could get yourself in a heap of trouble if you come on too strong one way or the other."

Simmonds was becoming impatient. "All right, table the internal communication issue for now. Let's talk shareholders. They aren't going to be too happy to hear about this. Remember that glowing profile of Ned in the trade magazine last year? Our shareholders think Ned is the only reason KTI is doing well. What do we say to reassure them that the competition doesn't have the upper hand? Dammit," Simmonds broke off his own train of thought. "I want to sue Ned."

"Our shareholders think Ned is the only reason KTI is doing well."

"You probably shouldn't," Craswell said. "Unfortunately, there isn't much legal basis on which to sue him. After all, he didn't have a noncompete clause in his employment contract. There is probable cause in the sense of misappropriation of goodwill, and we can take him to court on that. But there is no guarantee we would win."

"Should I ask my other vice presidents to sign non-compete clauses?" Simmonds asked.

"You could," Craswell said, "but that might signal panic in the chief executive's office. Noncompete clauses are uncommon in this industry. A move like that could end up generating a fair amount of resentment. What you might consider is working noncompete clauses into contracts for new people you hire into key positions."

"That would be a problem as well, though," Murray cut in. "A policy like that would make KTI much less attractive to the most qualified candidates. But I still think we're getting far off the track here. You're probably thinking that I'm negative about all your plans for action, but I do agree that we need a plan—and we need one immediately."

"Let's steal Diane Tucker away from Daltex," Simmonds said, smiling grimly. He held up a hand at Murray's frown. "I know, I know. I'm not being serious. But to be honest, I'm shook up about more than Ned. This used to be a collegial industry. We used to close deals on a handshake, share technologies, and hold trade shows that were as much fun for us as for any customer. Remember when we pooled resources to revive Standard Carpet after its main plant burned down? Daltex contributed to that effort as well. Nowadays you look around and see allegations of price-fixing. You hear rumors of industrial espionage and sabotage. I don't want to exacerbate the problems, but Daltex has, in effect, declared war on us with this move. How can we fight back?"

How Should KTI Respond to a Vice President's Defection?

Five experts consider damage-control strategies and legal issues.

KENNETH L. COLEMAN *is the senior vice president of administration at Silicon Graphics in Mountain View, California. His responsibilities include human resources, external affairs, information systems, corporate purchasing, corporate services, and facilities.*

I am amazed that Paul Simmonds, David Murray, and Rick Craswell are sitting around planning a course of action and trying to guess why Ned Carpenter is leaving without doing the obvious: talking to Carpenter. If I were the CEO, the head of human resources, or a third party in that morning meeting, I wouldn't assume Carpenter is out the door. Not yet. The first thing I would do is try having a conversation with him. After all, he is the only person who knows what's going on.

Too often in situations like this, people speculate about others' motivations instead of simply asking them. Much of the time, all the conjecture is way off base. Maybe Carpenter's decision isn't irrevocable. Maybe he doesn't truly want to leave but is looking for an indication that the company values him. Maybe he's angry about a particular incident. Maybe Daltex offered him a more lucrative compensation package. The point is that Simmonds, Murray, and Craswell won't know until they ask. They have everything to gain and nothing to lose by speaking with Carpenter face-to-face. I've found that most people leaving a company want their departures to be as friendly as possible and are willing to be quite open about what's on their minds.

Now, because Simmonds is difficult to work with at times—and because he seems upset about the situation—I suggest that Murray first talk to Carpenter. If Carpenter considers staying, he'll have to speak with Simmonds eventually, but someone who is more likely to remain calm should initiate the conversation. Murray should call Carpenter immediately and sit down with him as soon as possible. If Murray can persuade him to stay, so much the better. One bargaining chip KTI has over many of its competitors is the fact that it's publicly traded. If Carpenter's complaints are largely financial, Murray and Simmonds should consider offering him a compensation package that includes equity. The possibility of large financial rewards if KTI does well would be an excellent incentive for Carpenter to stay and to excel.

Murray must also be prepared to learn that Carpenter is set on leaving. In that case, KTI's top managers must deal with three important issues. First, Murray must ask Carpenter what his intentions are. Does he plan a friendly departure? If not, is there something specific Murray can help iron out? If Carpenter is truly leaving, the company's objective must be to make his departure as nonadversarial as possible. As I mentioned earlier, most people who resign want to leave a company on good terms. The company may be able to persuade Carpenter to agree—in writing or at least verbally—that he won't try to steal personnel and that he won't say anything negative about KTI.

Second, Murray and Simmonds must handle internal and external communications. They should draft a memo to all employees explaining what's happening and wishing Carpenter the best in his new job. They should also draft a press release, keeping the tone as friendly as possible. Ideally, the release would include a quote from Carpenter along these lines: "I'm leaving KTI for personal reasons, but I wish the company all the best. I believe in KTI, and I hope for its continued success." He is likely to cooperate.

Third, KTI's top managers must address the issue of Carpenter's replacement. Because John Brady does not seem perfect for the job, I think Simmonds and Murray must hold off on appointing him until they have spoken with his current peers and the people who will be his peers if he is promoted. Simmonds and Murray need to find out if the organization will support Brady as the vice president of operations. Jumping the gun won't serve KTI well. And talking to the employees who would be affected by Brady's promotion may uncover other solutions.

Finally, a quick mention of some things I would never do if I were Simmonds or Murray. I wouldn't sue Carpenter. If he has revealed the company's strategy for rolling out the new fiber coating, that would be another story. But in this instance, he probably hasn't done anything wrong, and KTI wouldn't win. Suing Carpenter would send the message that KTI doesn't trust its employees and assumes the worst about those who decide to leave. I prefer to act on the assumption that people want to do the right thing.

I also wouldn't ask anyone to sign a noncompete clause. In a field in which a relatively small number of cutthroat competitors control most of the market, a noncompete clause in effect tells people that if they leave a company they will never work in the industry again. That's not realistic.

Given that the CEO is suggesting flawed strategies such as lawsuits and noncompete clauses, I suspect KTI doesn't have a lot of open, honest communication channels. The symptoms are clear: Simmonds has a problem delegating, no one knows why Carpenter is leaving, and no one really knows if Brady would be right for the job. After this crisis has passed, Murray must try to help open up communication at KTI. As the head of human resources, he is responsible for doing so. And if he is able to knock down some of the walls inside the company, he may help prevent problems in the future. KTI seems to have potential. It would be a shame to let a narrow-minded, defensive culture bring the company down.

STEPHEN A. GREYSER *is the Richard P. Chapman Professor at the Harvard Business School in Boston, Mas-*

*sachusetts. He specializes in corporate communications
and consumer marketing. His longtime association with
HBR includes service as an editor, research director, and
secretary and chairman of the editorial board. He is a
director of Edelman Worldwide Public Relations and several other companies.*

Simmonds and KTI face two sets of challenges. One is
the need to reassure KTI's stakeholders that the company remains strong and directed. The other is the need
to live up to those assurances.

Craswell is right that Carpenter's departure will be
news in the Dalton area almost immediately. The word
will also spread rapidly in the carpet industry, especially
given its geographic concentration. Simmonds must
quickly prepare comments for the local paper and TV
and radio stations and for the trade press.

He must think carefully about the key messages he
wants to communicate and the external and internal
target audiences to whom those messages should be
addressed. Simmonds must not allow anger or the desire
for revenge to control his words. Instead, he should
express regret over Carpenter's departure and low-key
recognition of his contributions.

Simmonds's principal message should be that the
company is committed to continuity. The public needs
to hear that the strategy and initiatives that led to KTI's
recent success will not change just because Carpenter is
leaving. To support that message, Simmonds can stress
that the company's program of change is not only still
under way but also on schedule. He can also mention
that KTI is making great strides in developing new
products. Both initiatives are probably well known, but

there is no reason not to mention them again and emphasize their value. Reporters from the trade press are more likely than others to ask questions about new products and the future of the program, especially because coverage of KTI has highlighted Carpenter as an engine of the company's success. Reporters from the local media are more likely to explore the personal—and personality—aspects of the story. Simmonds should be ready to field both types of questions.

He also has to be prepared to tell reporters who is going to replace Carpenter. If Brady is the person for the job, announcing his appointment would strengthen KTI's continuity message. If Simmonds decides that Brady is not necessarily the right person but is capable of managing operations for now, that arrangement should be announced but not trumpeted. If Brady is leaving KTI, Simmonds must announce the immediate start of a search to fill Carpenter's and Brady's positions, and he must underscore the company's commitment to making the transitions as smooth as possible.

Internally, Simmonds must talk with KTI's senior executives right away in order to stimulate the teamwork the company needs in the wake of Carpenter's departure. Simmonds should also schedule individual meetings in the next day or two to discuss each manager's role in the company and to assure each executive of his or her importance to KTI.

In an effort to short-circuit the rumor mill, Simmonds also needs to communicate with the rest of KTI's employees. He can do so in a memo circulated by E-mail and also posted in the company's cafeteria and on departmental bulletin boards. The memo should briefly report Carpenter's resignation, express regret, and remind everyone of the commitment to continuity.

Customers are another important audience. Although many will read about Carpenter's departure in trade publications, a message from KTI's marketing department or salespeople wouldn't hurt. Customers usually do not deal directly with a company's operations, however, so the message should be matter-of-fact. There is no need to suggest that customers should be concerned about Carpenter's departure.

Finally, because KTI is a public company, Simmonds must inform and reassure key institutional shareholders. For broader financial markets, a brief announcement of the resignation and the continuity message should suffice. KTI is not among the large conglomerates that participate in the industry, but the company's CFO still should be prepared to handle a reaction from Wall Street and to field analysts' calls.

All the above communication is essential. But communications are claims; they become credible only through a company's behavior. If Simmonds touts the company's commitment to continuity, he must make sure that it continues to operate in a healthy fashion. If Brady is to be the next vice president of operations, he should be settled into the role as quickly as possible. If

Noncompete clauses do not provide any protection against defection.

Brady is not the person for the job, the search for a successor must be a priority. Before Carpenter was hired, KTI may have interviewed candidates from outside and inside the industry who are still interested. The search may not be starting from scratch.

Simmonds, Craswell, and Murray suggest other possible actions: suing Carpenter, seeking noncompete agreements from current and prospective managers, and escalating a war with Daltex. All those tactics, in my opinion, not only digress from the main task but also could damage KTI, especially in the short run. Simmonds must keep the following points in mind:

- A lawsuit would be a public sign of retaliation against Carpenter as well as Daltex, even if Daltex is not named. Besides, according to the corporate counsel, KTI has no basis for a suit. The company would do better to signal privately to Carpenter—perhaps in a note expressing regret about his resignation—that KTI expects him to keep the company's trade secrets.

- Noncompete clauses provide no protection against defection. If such clauses are not common in the industry, KTI should not initiate them at a time of perceived weakness. They are threatening, and they generally require some give on the company's part. Right now, KTI is probably not prepared to negotiate guaranteed contracts and the other benefits that employees might demand if asked to sign noncompete agreements. The company must focus on building morale, not on setting new policy based on anger.

- A war would only make it more difficult to survive in an already difficult industry. In Simmonds's view, the situation is like Fort Sumter: "Daltex has declared war on us." That is a dangerous attitude, especially in light of the industry's thin profits and the deep pockets of KTI's largest competitors. KTI may be in for the kind of competitive intensity we see in the "eternal duel" between Coke and Pepsi. And right now, the company doesn't seem capable of sustaining such a battle. Besides, in Dalton, it is likely that the industry's leaders belong to the same clubs, eat at the same restaurants, work on the same community causes, and see one another at social functions. Does Simmonds really want to engage in a battle? His energies would be better focused on KTI's internal business problems.

Finally, Simmonds should look in the mirror. Is he too quick to anger? Did he ignore signs of Carpenter's unhappiness? Were the heated conversations about the markets for the fiber coating necessary? Did Carpenter's grumblings about compensation reflect deeper discontent? Overall, did Simmonds take Carpenter for granted?

The answers to those questions—and Simmonds's ability to address the personal issues they raise—are significant. Simmonds must heed Craswell's admonition to think straight and act on what he discovers. If he does not, Carpenter's departure may be the first of many, and KTI's future will be in jeopardy.

HAL BURLINGAME *is the executive vice president of human resources at AT&T Corporation in Basking Ridge, New Jersey.*

Simmonds has to accomplish several tasks concurrently in order to get on top of the situation at KTI. He has to stabilize the team responsible for the change program, formulate and implement a communications strategy for the press and for shareholders, and figure out how to deal with Carpenter and with Daltex. On all fronts, he must lead from strength, not from angst.

Simmonds's first task is to prepare all KTI employees for the change and make sure that they hear about Carpenter's departure before the press does. A critical part of that task is gathering together the people responsible for implementing KTI's change program and reassuring them that they are still valued members of the company. Simmonds must make it clear to them that he knows Carpenter was their leader but that he has confidence in their ability and motivation to carry on and to excel. If necessary, Simmonds can offer additional compensation to strengthen his message.

As for a new team leader, I don't see any overwhelming evidence in Brady's favor. Simmonds should identify some external candidates for the position. KTI found Carpenter through an outside search not too long ago; it shouldn't be difficult to do the sweep again. Simmonds then must take the time to weigh the external candidates against internal ones, including Brady. Simmonds would be better off having the team report directly to him for a while than appointing someone without careful consideration. KTI is not up against a wall; Simmonds shouldn't act as if it were.

I would communicate the same message to the press and to shareholders that I sent to people inside the company: Carpenter was the leader of the team, but he was by no means the only valuable member. Simmonds can acknowledge that Carpenter was a strong player and say that he is sorry to see a competitor get any KTI employee, but he shouldn't belabor the point. Instead, he should demonstrate that KTI is ready and able to continue the progress it has made, at the same pace and with the same attention to quality. He might consider introducing several team members to the press and to industry analysts. He can talk about the qualifications of those employees and the responsibilities they have had throughout the change program, and about how pleased the company is to have such a strong team in place. Beyond that, Simmonds should keep a relatively low profile in the coming weeks. This crisis will pass, and if the change program stays on course and on schedule, the company can announce its progress along the way.

Above all, Simmonds should be careful not to reveal his feelings about Carpenter or let the threat of shareholders' displeasure ruin his perspective. Yes, he is very angry right now, and, yes, KTI's stock price may fall a bit. But trashing Carpenter and acting defensively about the company's market performance will only turn a potential weakness into a real one.

What about Carpenter and Daltex? KTI's counsel should take action immediately to ensure that Carpenter isn't in a position to take KTI's secrets—or personnel— to his new employer. It may be unusual in the carpet industry, but most companies in KTI's position would contact the company in Daltex's position to negotiate an agreement. Simmonds and Craswell shouldn't wait. Carpenter's departure could represent a serious threat to KTI, and although internal and external communications must be positive, that's no reason to treat legal issues casually. KTI must destroy Daltex's leverage and Carpenter's capacity to steal KTI's best people.

Simmonds, Craswell, and Murray seem to be letting Carpenter's resignation paralyze them. Now is not the time for inaction and indecision. The sooner they realize that Carpenter doesn't control their actions, the sooner KTI can emerge from this crisis and get on with the business of growing the business.

ROB GALFORD *lives in Concord, Massachusetts, and works with senior managers on performance, organizational, and career issues. He also teaches in executive education programs at Columbia University's Graduate*

School of Business in New York City and at Northwestern University's J.L. Kellogg Graduate School of Management in Evanston, Illinois.

Simmonds, for all his talents as a CEO, has certainly let himself be blindsided. He didn't do much in the way of contingency planning, given the no longer snug-as-a-bug world of carpets in Dalton, Georgia. In that competitive environment, it's hard to believe that this is the first time a senior executive in the industry has jumped ship. Why wasn't Simmonds aware of the possibility? This sort of stuff happens all the time. And noncompete clauses and hardball litigation are only partial deterrents. But, as my grandmother used to say, "Man plans and God laughs." So, now that we have taken Simmonds to task for putting KTI on the high wire without a net, what can we do to help the guy?

Before Simmonds does anything else, he must get a jump on the news. Specific steps should include the following:

- issuing a press release announcing Carpenter's departure, acknowledging his contributions, and wishing him well;

- placing a few calls to important customers and the media to tell them personally of the resignation and to show that the company deals well with change;

- meeting first with the senior staff and then with the employees as a group to demonstrate how to take this kind of event in stride and to remind everyone that they are talented and capable;

- spending some time one-on-one with Brady and other important KTI players; and

- taking a few moments to consider how his own behavior might have hastened Carpenter's departure.

After this first round of damage control, Simmonds must address several issues. First, he doesn't have to promote Brady to Carpenter's position in a nanosecond. Brady's qualifications as Carpenter's second-in-command put him in the running, but it would be valuable to consider what the role of the vice president of operations *is* as well as what it *needs to be*. Carpenter obviously had the right skills to get a change program off the ground, but maybe the later stages of the program call for someone with a different set of skills or someone who can sustain the level of enthusiasm that Carpenter brought to the task. It's also worthwhile to keep in mind that Carpenter himself was an industry outsider (dare we say carpetbagger?) a mere three years ago, that his learning curve was steep, and that his performance was exceptional. Another talented individual could learn how to perform in the role just as he did. Simmonds should announce the start of a search immediately, give Brady a fair shot, and let the search professionals do their best. The shareholders will probably give KTI a knock no matter how the company responds to the crisis, but attempting to cure the problem too quickly or with the wrong medicine could give shareholders even more reasons to object later on.

Second, Simmonds could well afford to get closer to employees at all levels of the company. Murray must gather some courage and figure out how to communicate that to the CEO. Simmonds is not always an easy guy to work with. Does he acknowledge that? Has he given his employees explicit messages that he values their best thinking? Does he know if his style or listening skills prevent him from getting the best from his employees?

Becoming more intimate with employees—and developing some humility—might not have kept Carpenter from leaving, but maybe it's not too late to keep some of his colleagues from doing the same.

Finally, and perhaps most important, Simmonds needs an adviser. His situation serves as a clear reminder of the value of a confidant to a CEO or to any senior executive, for that matter. In my work, I have found that senior managers can be the loneliest people in the business world. The need to appear decisive, the competitive races they often run with people in their organizations, and the turmoil of their lives do not give them many opportunities to reflect or to express fear, doubt, and uncertainty. There aren't always lots of people around in whom they feel they can confide.

Although Murray is a "trusted lieutenant," he is an insider, which may make it difficult for him to offer dispassionate advice or a fresh perspective. Good advisers can be colleagues, but more often they are independent consultants to the company or to the individual: a partner in a law office, a consulting firm, or an accounting practice, for example, or even an outside director on the company's board. Such people can—in forthright, judicious terms—listen to and talk with someone like Simmonds about what's going well, what's weighing heavily, when to get off the high horse, and when to take action. If Simmonds had had an adviser like that in the first place, he might be having coffee with Carpenter right now at the Broadloom Breakfast Joint.

GREGORY S. RUBIN *is the senior attorney at Rubin & Associates, a law firm in Paoli, Pennsylvania, that specializes in drafting and enforcing postemployment restrictive covenants and corporate policies to protect trade secrets. In the past 15 years, the firm has litigated at least 2,000 cases in 48 states.*

Carpenter has the keys to the kingdom. He knows which doors they open and what's behind each door. And from all indications, he wasn't too happy with Simmonds or with KTI in the months before his abrupt departure. Unhappy or not, he could do a lot of damage. But yesterday afternoon, last night, and half of the morning have passed, and no one at KTI knows what Carpenter is up to. The company didn't even conduct an exit interview with him before he left the premises. KTI has slept on its rights.

Now the company must act quickly. It should be Murray, not the CEO, who takes the lead. Whoever talks to Carpenter and to Daltex now must be prepared to spend time submitting an affidavit in court and even serving as KTI's key witness throughout lengthy litigation. First, Murray should call Carpenter and ask him to come back for an exit interview. If he declines, Murray should try to conduct the interview over the phone. He must be nonthreatening but still get the answers to some important questions: Does Carpenter have any papers and computer disks that contain KTI's corporate information? Is his new job going to require him to disclose KTI's trade secrets? Will he be soliciting KTI's employees or customers?

After that interview, Murray should call Carpenter's new boss and cover the same ground. If Carpenter reveals to Murray that he has betrayed KTI, Murray must push Daltex to corroborate that. He should also try to get answers from Carpenter and from Daltex in writing. If either party objects or asks why, he should explain that KTI's lawyers need that information. Throughout all this,

Murray must keep in mind that questions, not accusations, are the order of the day. Carpenter may not have done anything wrong, and KTI is looking for answers, not a lawsuit for defamation.

The next step is to make it ab-solutely clear to Carpenter that he may not use or disclose KTI's confidential business information. The information about KTI's new fiber coating and the upcoming commercial launch—and basically everything else Carpenter learned about KTI while he worked there—is confidential and KTI's exclusive property. Even if that message has already been conveyed to Carpenter and Daltex verbally, KTI should state it again in a letter. (See "Dear Ned" at the end of this article.) Murray should fax that letter, mail it, *and* deliver it in person to Carpenter at Daltex. And while he's there, he should look around for documents that belong to KTI. If he sees any, he should demand their return. He shouldn't breach the peace, but it's okay to let Carpenter know that KTI is serious about protecting its information.

Once Murray has done those tasks, he and Simmonds should meet with key personnel. The company needs their help—and perhaps their testimony. What do those people know about Carpenter's departure? Have any documents been stolen, copied, or destroyed? Have any computer data been encrypted, erased, or altered? Did Carpenter try to lure any of KTI's employees to Daltex?

Given the information revealed in the case, KTI does not have grounds for a good lawsuit. Carpenter has not signed a noncompete or even a nondisclosure agreement. And there are no facts, circumstances, prior dealings, or any other evidence from which a court could infer a quasi contract. Had KTI established a policy for the protection of its trade secrets in its employee hand-book, company manual, guidelines for business conduct, corporate resolutions, compliance rules, memos from the president, bulletins, minutes of sales meetings, or employee publications, it might have a case. But it didn't and it doesn't. Carpenter is free to join Daltex and start work right away. At-will employment means just that.

But if Carpenter or Daltex has misappropriated any KTI trade secrets, then KTI can obtain a temporary restraining order. If Carpenter has crossed any line, it's most likely that he has violated the Uniform Trade Secret Act, which applies in 41 states, including Georgia. If KTI seeks to enjoin Carpenter from using or disclosing the information he acquired during his employment at KTI, the company will have the burden of showing that the information he has is a trade secret protected by law and that there is a legal basis—either a covenant or a confi-dential relationship—on which to take action. Assuming there is no contract, expressed or implied, the court would consider factors such as the extent to which the information is known outside KTI's industry; the extent to which it is known by other employees at KTI; the extent of measures taken by the company to guard the secrecy of the information; the value of the information to KTI and to competitors such as Daltex; the amount of effort or money expended by KTI to develop the informa-tion; and the ease or difficulty with which the informa-tion could be legitimately acquired or duplicated.

If Carpenter, while still employed at KTI, disclosed confidential information to outsiders, conspired with a group of fellow employees, told customers he was mov-ing to Daltex or asked them to move with him, defamed the company, or engaged in acts of unfair competition designed to cripple KTI, the company could proceed on those grounds, too.

Meanwhile, Simmonds shouldn't hire Diane Tucker from Daltex. What's more, he shouldn't attempt any damage control until he knows if there is damage to control. If reporters call, he must be ready to say, "We confirm Carpenter's change of employment and wish him well" or "KTI has filed an action with the court, and the company does not comment on matters in litigation." But he shouldn't alert the media himself. He also shouldn't say anything to most of KTI's employees except that the company is sorry to see Carpenter leave and will announce any new changes.

As for the future, Simmonds needs to recognize that the days of collegiality in the carpet industry are probably over. The stakes are too high and the temptations too great. In most cases, the Carpenters of the world walk off with customer lists, pricing and marketing plans, and other information that competitors can use to cut throats.

KTI doesn't necessarily need noncompete agreements. The company's primary objective is not to prevent former employees from working in the carpet industry but to keep confidential information from getting into the wrong hands. The company would have a lot less to worry about if it had a written corporate policy on trade secrets and if its managers agreed to reasonable postemployment restrictive covenants, such as nondisclosure and nonsolicitation agreements. Most large companies use such restrictions; why shouldn't KTI?

It's time for contracts, confidentiality agreements, and an explicit statement of corporate policy. It's also time to look for a new counsel. Replace Rick Craswell with a dog that can hunt.

Dear Ned:

I WAS SORRY THAT I did not have advance notice of
your resignation. As you know, on a personal level, you
will be greatly missed. On a professional level, your contributions to our R&D and marketing efforts and your
knowledge of our internal operations made you one of
our most valuable assets. For those reasons, we ask you to
reconsider your resignation and come back to KTI. I am
available to meet with you at any time. Please call me.

In the event that you stay on at Daltex, you should be
aware that the information you acquired at KTI is confidential and the sole and exclusive property of KTI. That
information was entrusted to you as a fiduciary of the
company and is not to be disclosed to any third party,
including your current employer, now or at any time. If
you have possession of, access to, or control over such
information, please return it immediately to KTI. Please do
not disclose or divulge such information to any third
party, including Daltex. If you have already done so,
please retrieve such information and have Daltex or any
other third party purge the information from its system.
Please refrain from any future use or disclosure of such
information.

Furthermore, we ask that you faithfully discharge your
fiduciary duty and your duty of loyalty to KTI by not soliciting for hire any of our current or recent employees. If
you have already engaged in such solicitation, please
cease and desist.

Finally, do not solicit for your own benefit or for the
benefit of Daltex the patronage of any KTI account, customer, or prospective customer with whom you dealt at
KTI or whose identity you learned while employed by

KTI. If you have already done so, please refrain from accepting business from or conducting business with those accounts.

KTI requires absolute and strict compliance with the above. We seek your assurance and the assurance of Daltex that you both will comply in every respect. Please provide Daltex with a copy of this letter so it, too, may confirm its compliance. You both may do so by signing the enclosed copy of this letter where indicated and returning it to me. Your failure to do so may require KTI to seek the assistance of the courts to enjoin and restrain any of the above-referenced prohibited conduct.

I look forward to your prompt reply to this letter and hope that you, I, KTI, and Daltex will continue to have collegial personal and corporate relationships.

Very truly yours,

Paul Simmonds

AGREED TO:

_____Ned Carpenter

_____President of Daltex

Attest:_____

Originally published in January–February 1997
Reprint 97111

HBR's cases present common managerial dilemmas and offer concrete solutions from experts. As written, they are hypothetical, and the names used are fictitious.

A Strategic Approach to Managing Product Recalls

N. CRAIG SMITH,

ROBERT J. THOMAS, AND

JOHN A. QUELCH

Executive Summary

PRODUCT RECALLS CAN DESTROY BRANDS and even companies. But according to the authors, if a company handles recalls strategically, it can lessen their negative impact and maybe even reap some benefits.

The authors maintain that a strategic approach to recalls should address the implications of a recall for all relevant business functions and should deal with all stages of a recall, from readiness before the fact to product reintroduction after a recall has ended. The authors offer step-by-step guidelines on handling recalls effectively. Among their recommendations:

- Create a recall response team to evaluate potential recall situations, to decide on an appropriate response, to oversee the response, and to bring the recall to a close.

- Design products and conduct product testing with recalls in mind. Thorough testing can uncover potential problems before a product is marketed, and designing products with features such as built-in traceability makes handling a recall easier.

- Establish and maintain channels of communication. The communications function keeps all concerned parties informed during a recall and can take advantage of positive responses to a well-handled recall by publicizing them.

- Stage mock recalls to test how well logistics and information systems actually perform. Logistics and information systems provide the physical backbone for a smooth recall process.

With forethought and planning, the authors assert, unavoidable recalls can have long-term favorable outcomes.

In November 1994, Intel Corporation was confronted by angry customers demanding replacement of their Pentium microprocessors, which had been reported to have a flaw affecting mathematical calculations. The company's first response was to demand that customers demonstrate that their chips were faulty; only then would Intel issue replacements. Intel claimed that the flaw was unlikely to affect most users—that it occurred only once in every 9 billion random calculations—but consumer confidence in the product already had begun to waiver. The company stubbornly held its ground for more than a month in the face of a storm of protest. Then IBM, a major purchaser of the Pentium micropro-

cessor, halted shipments of its computers containing the chip. At last, on the brink of market disaster, Intel instituted a no-questions-asked returns policy.

Chastened, CEO Andrew Grove later said, "We got caught between our mindset, which is a fact-based, analysis-based engineer's mindset, and [the] customers' mindset, which is not so much emotional but accustomed to making their own choice."[1] He also noted that "the kernel of the issue we missed . . . was that we presumed to tell somebody what they should or shouldn't worry about, or should or shouldn't do." The cost of the recall was estimated at close to $500 million. Grove, usually held in high regard by Wall Street and the business press, had learned about recalls the hard way.

P RODUCT RECALLS ARE increasing. In 1988, the U.S. Consumer Product Safety Commission was involved in some 221 recalls covering about 8 million product units. Five years later, in 1993, those numbers had risen to 367 recalls covering about 28 million product units. Recalls for both new and established products occur all too often, and they can have serious repercussions. In some cases, they have destroyed brands and even companies.

So why aren't more companies prepared to deal with recalls? In part, it's because they don't recognize how great an impact a recall can have on an organization's reputation. In part, it's an issue of time: in the frenzy of a product launch, the last thing most managers think about is how to get a new product back if something goes wrong. But even those managers who believe that their companies are prepared to handle a recall rarely understand what successful recall management entails.

They may have a rudimentary plan for dealing with customers and with the press and a general idea of how internal communications should be handled in the event of a recall, but those preparations fall far short of constituting a plan that will truly minimize the damage threatened by a recall.

What's needed is a strategy that cuts across the company, addressing the implications of a recall for all relevant business functions. The strategy also should cut across time, dealing with all stages of the recall. For the purposes of discussion, we have delineated the following functional areas: policy and planning, product development, communications, and logistics and information systems. A company's plan must prepare each of those areas for the three phases of the recall: the discovery of the problem, the recall itself, and the aftermath and follow-up actions. (See the exhibit "A User's Guide to Managing Product Recalls.")

We have studied how companies have handled a recall, and, in the light of our observations of those that have emerged unscathed, we have created a framework to help managers assess their current recall strategy and design a plan tailored to their company's needs.

The Returns of Sound Recall Management

If product recalls are handled properly, a company not only can keep damage to a minimum but also may find opportunities to reap unexpected benefits. Consider Saturn Corporation's early recall experience. A month after the first Saturns were launched, the company discovered a flaw in the car's front-seat recliner mechanisms. As soon as it had tracked down the problem, Saturn voluntarily recalled 1,480 cars. After briefing dealers on the recall by closed-circuit television, the company contacted all customers by letter through an overnight delivery service and told them whether or not their car was affected. The recall went so smoothly that the company incorporated it in its advertising campaign. One ad showed a Saturn representative flying to Alaska with a replacement seat. That car had been purchased elsewhere because there were no dealers in Alaska: the ad showed how far out of its way Saturn would go to satisfy customers.

Granted, the scope of Saturn's recall was small by most standards, but the company would not have been able to coordinate its manufacturing, service, communications, and marketing activities as readily as it did if it had not been prepared with a recall-management strategy. In fact, Saturn had decided how to respond to a recall more than a year before the October 1990 launch of its first car. Managers knew that the company's success depended on building long-term relationships with customers and dealers, and that anything that could jeopardize those relationships—such as a recall—would have to be dealt with quickly and effectively. And they recognized the value of a recall plan that could complement the company's marketing efforts. In effect, Saturn's approach to the recall and the company's subsequent actions were part of its business strategy, and the strategy paid off.

Intuit's experience in 1995 is another good example of successful recall management. During the 1995 tax season, a user of Intuit's tax software found errors in some of the program's computations. He called the company's customer-service department but was unhappy with the service he received, so he told his story to the *San Francisco Chronicle*. Publication of the story led to national

A User's Guide to Managing Product Recalls

Business Function	Phase of the Recall (and Outcome Sought)		
	Before	During	After
	(Readiness for recalls)	(Sound recall management)	(All stakeholders recognize recall's success)
Policy and Planning	· Foster recognition of the importance of recall readiness. · Assign recall responsibility. · Develop (and review) recall manuals.	· Establish recall response team and determine seriousness of recall. · Decide type of recall and scale of response. · Develop recall plan and build commitment to it. · Plan product reintroduction.	· Design resolution plan to close effort. · Complete (and implement) plan for product reintroduction. · Audit recall. · Congratulate recall response team and thank participants.
Product Development	· Promote TQM, product testing, and study of yesterday's products. · Explicitly consider product safety and traceability in new-product development. · Take possibility of recalls into account during new-product development.	· Determine cause of defect. · Determine adjustment offer, including product replacement. · Fix design flaws responsible for defect.	· Identify glitches in development process that led to product defect. · Monitor customer satisfaction with product replacement and reintroduced product.

Communications	· Identify recall stakeholders. · Build organization's credibility in the eyes of stakeholders. · Incorporate recall into corporate crisis-communications plan.	· Quickly communicate awareness of problem and company responses to stakeholders. · Select media and decide on messages. · Announce recall. · Report recall progress.	· Reassure customers and other stakeholders. · Tell success stories. · Rebuild or augment brand franchise through advertising and promotions.
Logistics and information systems	· Provide for rapid notification of product defects. · Test product traceability. · Design systems to handle recalls. · Consider staging mock recall to test systems.	· Trace product. · Set up recall-management information systems and logistics.	· Maintain recall logistics beyond recall. · Document recall notification procedures. · Identify possible improvements in recall logistics and information systems.

coverage of the problem. Upon hearing the story and investigating the problem, Intuit's chairman, Scott Cook, quickly announced that the company's 1995 tax-year software contained bugs. He then offered a corrected replacement disk to those who requested it and wrote a personal letter of apology to the company's 1.65 million

Both Saturn and Intuit reacted to recalls strategically—and emerged stronger for it.

users, saying that the company had really let its customers down. In a display of trust, Intuit placed the corrected version of the software on major on-line services for anyone to copy and also offered refunds to customers who requested them. The company was able to avert a market backlash, in large part thanks to its quick and effective management of the situation. In fact, one major software retailer was quoted as saying, "It's been business as usual, which has been surprising."[2]

Saturn had a sound recall-management plan in place; Intuit, apparently, did not. But in both cases, senior managers quickly confessed their mistakes and sought to make amends with appropriate corrections. Both companies reacted strategically, focusing on long-term marketing implications, and both emerged stronger for the experience. Intel, on the other hand, initially reacted to its Pentium crisis tactically, focusing on the technical aspects of the problem, and it did not weather the recall storm particularly well.

Preparing for a Recall

How can a company prepare itself properly for a recall that it doesn't even know will happen? Each of the four

functions delineated earlier must make advance preparations, must react appropriately during the recall, and
must take the right steps afterward.

POLICY AND PLANNING (OVERALL COORDINATION OF A RECALL)

Long before a recall becomes necessary, senior managers
should be fostering an organizationwide recognition of
the need for recall readiness. They should ensure that
employees understand the link between recalls and consumer safety and satisfaction, as well as the effect well-
run recalls can have on corporate success. They also
should fight any signs of a "kill the messenger" culture
that might prevent news of a product's problems from
reaching the appropriate people. Thought of broadly,
this task is difficult—a company's culture does not
become "open" overnight, and it isn't easy to identify
weaknesses in the chain of communication when it is
not being tested with a real-life situation. But there are a
number of steps managers can take to move their companies in the right direction.

First, the overall responsibility for product recalls
should be assigned to one senior executive. It might be
the senior vice president for marketing, another senior
vice president, or even the CEO, depending on the size of
the company, its organizational structure, and its individual circumstances. That manager should require the
development (and regular review) of a recall manual that
details the company's policy and guidelines in the event
of a recall. The material in the manual should derive
from marketing; in effect, a recall operation is based on a
reverse-marketing plan. Customer satisfaction and other

marketing goals remain paramount; however, the task is to use marketing skills to *retrieve* the product from the customer.

In creating a recall-ready organization, the person with overall responsibility should identify key managers throughout the organization who might be called on to act in a recall situation. The idea is to avoid blindsiding anyone. Some companies also enlist the help of people outside the organization in anticipation of a recall. The vice president of marketing for Netscape Communications Corporation offered cash or prizes to anyone— inside or outside the company—who found problems in a test version of its software designed for browsing the Internet.

In the event of a recall, the senior recall manager should appoint a response team, including a "recall champion," to manage the recall on a daily basis. The response team should be made up of those people the manager has tapped in advance from the various areas in the company. The team members' first task is to establish the seriousness of the situation. Such an evaluation will help them determine the speed and type of response and will be especially useful when there is a risk of customer injury or illness. An incorrect assessment of the severity of the problem can lead to lasting trouble.

It is critical to arrive at a decision regarding a recall as swiftly as possible.

After the team evaluates the situation, it should determine the scale of the response necessary. It should also decide what type of recall is warranted. Does the situation require a full recall, a selective recall, a repair or retrofit offer, an optional recall, or a change in the production and distribution of the product? Can the problem be solved by offering customers an opportunity to exchange the product or by issuing an advisory? If a government agency has called for the recall, is it truly warranted? Are the charges accurate? Should the company refute them? If recall action is warranted, the response team should also determine the announcement (who will make it; when and where; who should be notified; and what the script will be) and coordinate the field response program (who will be accepting the faulty products; how the company plans to monitor the products that have been returned; and who will be providing repairs or replacements).

The team should keep in mind that it is critical to arrive at a decision regarding the recall as swiftly as possible. But a decision doesn't necessarily have to mean taking action. A recall made too soon could give credibility to an unsubstantiated charge. In 1993, for example, the Pepsi-Cola Company was confronted with the possibility of a recall when reports that syringes had been found in its canned cola beverages led to rumors that someone was tampering with the products prior to sale. The data that Pepsi quickly accumulated following those reports did not, however, confirm the rumors. Although Pepsi, in cooperation with the U.S. Food and Drug Administration, launched a public relations campaign to inform consumers of the need for caution, authorities soon discovered that the syringes were being inserted after sale by unscrupulous individuals. Pepsi's managers did not launch a recall, and their decision was a good one. In Pepsi's case, an immediate decision to recall the product would have been far more costly to the company, its customers, and other stakeholders than the course taken.

Another factor militating against hasty recall action is the company's liability exposure. Although delaying the recall of an unsafe product may increase the size and number of claims against the company—not to mention potentially endangering consumers and creating ill will—issuing a recall amounts to admitting that there is a problem and may open the door to a flood of lawsuits. The recall response team should weigh all factors carefully before making a decision.

The management task is no less important after a recall. The response team should design a resolution plan to bring the effort to a satisfactory close. Team members must set goals for closure; for example, a given proportion of distributed units returned. And they must anticipate stragglers. If the recall process is effectively shut down, how will the company deal with an unhappy consumer who somehow missed the boat?

The team should also figure out how to reintroduce the product to the market. A reintroduction plan— which ideally would be developed and implemented with the participation of several of the people who originally designed and launched the product—might include a relaunch marketing effort to reassert brand identity and to build share.

And team members should keep an eye on the competition. In 1990, as Source Perrier labored to recall its bottled water globally because of reports that it contained benzene, rivals gained ground. Perrier's vulnerability contributed to Evian's emergence as a major player in the market and also gave new life to San Pelegrino, LaCroix, and others.

Finally, the recall team should audit the recall. There is a lot to be learned from how a company's recall plan worked in practice. What gave rise to the recall? What factors influenced its effectiveness and success? By conducting a review after the fact, managers can identify strengths and weaknesses of the effort and plan for a more effective response should another recall situation arise in the future.

When the recall is over, the recall champion should recognize and reward the major participants, especially members of the response team. During the recall, most team members will have had to perform their regular duties under intense time pressure or be covered by other personnel. Because a recall can have dire consequences for a company, one might think it would not be necessary to motivate a recall team. However, recalls are often conducted over several months and can become exhausting. Rewarding all participants, including retailers, is critical as well. For example, if a retailer played a major role in facilitating the process, the company might consider—within the constraints of the law—allowing preferential access to any of its products that are in short supply.

Poor recall policy and planning can have devastating consequences, even if it turns out the product is not at fault.

Mishandling the policy and planning side of a recall can have devastating consequences, even when it turns out that the product is not at fault. Witness the experience of Audi of America. In 1986, Audi was pressured to respond to a recall request made by the Center for Auto Safety (a group founded by consumer activist Ralph Nader) to the U.S. National Highway Traffic Safety Administration (NHTSA). A number of incidents involving injury and death had been reported in which Audi 5000s apparently surged out of control when drivers shifted from park to drive or reverse on their automatic transmissions. At the time, it was not clear if these unintended acceleration problems were caused by a technical flaw or by drivers' inability to manipulate the accelerator and brake pedals properly. (In most European cars, the pedals are located closer together than they are in American cars.)

Audi delayed its response for three months. Then it announced that it would replace the idle stabilization valve and relocate the brake and gas pedals on 132,000 Audi 5000s from the years 1984 through 1986. However, in its July 1986 recall, instead of performing those tasks, Audi installed a gear shift lock that required drivers to depress the brake before shifting into gear.

The cost of the recall to Audi was estimated at $25 million, which is typical of costs for automotive recalls of that scale. However, subsequent adverse television reports, a continual stream of accident reports—even on those models with the newly installed locks—and a class action suit devastated Audi's U.S. sales and its brand image. In fact, a 1990 study by Mary Sullivan in the *Journal of Business* revealed that the sudden acceleration problem was associated with a depreciation in the Audi 5000's resale value that was 11.5% greater than otherwise would have been the case. The publicity also lowered the resale value of other Audi models; for example, the Audi 4000 depreciated 9.2% more than forecast. Even the Audi Quattro, which did not have an automatic transmission, depreciated 6.8% more than expected in 1987.

Follow-up actions such as resale-value assurance programs, advertising, and sales promotions helped to recover some sales, but at a high cost. Then, in March 1989, a report by the NHTSA revealed that the sudden acceleration problem was due to driver error, not to a mechanical cause. But even that information did not reverse Audi's fortunes. The company's U.S. sales fell from some 74,000 units in 1985 to 21,225 units in 1989. And Audi continues to fare poorly. It will take a long time to rebuild consumer confidence in the brand and company—an expensive outcome to a situation that was not even caused by a mechanical flaw.

PRODUCT DEVELOPMENT

In Audi's case, poor policy and planning led to severe damage. In most cases, though, the culprit is, in fact, a faulty product. With hindsight, we can see that many recalls could have been avoided through a stronger commitment to product design and quality. But hindsight can become foresight when organizations acknowledge the possibility of a recall, particularly in their TQM and new-product development processes.

Braun, for instance, avoided a recall through comprehensive prelaunch product testing. When Braun was developing the KF40 coffeemaker, it designed a new handle for the glass carafe that was glued on rather than attached by a metal band. However, design engineers were concerned about the ability of an adhesive to survive heat and extended use. Sure enough, despite successful testing of prototypes, the glued plastic handles became detached on a few of the carafes when used by potential customers during prelaunch tests. Braun then redesigned the handle with a stylized hook over the top lip of the carafe to help keep the handle secure. Subsequent testing validated the new design. The product was launched in 1984 and became an instant and long-running success, selling 13.6 million units by the end of 1991. Anticipation of the problem with the handle, *additional* careful testing, and the ensuing redesign averted a potentially costly and damaging situation.

The likelihood of recalls can be reduced if senior managers can ensure that product design and quality—especially when safety-related—are comprehensively addressed throughout and beyond the new-product development process. The product development team should be constantly reviewing the track records of older products. Were there any recalls? Safety concerns? Was the product easy to repair? Such reviews help managers anticipate potential recall problems; they also help companies conduct more precise tests on new products.

Home-use testing can identify problems that arise through consumer use (and misuse).

And, although testing products is standard practice, there is a good deal to be gained from taking the product-testing process a step or two beyond the lab, as Braun did. A variety of use-oriented product-testing procedures can help identify and resolve defects. Braun's test of the coffee carafe with potential users early in the development process is an example of beta testing. Home-use testing often can identify safety hazards or other quality problems that may arise through consumer use (and misuse) of products and that can be fixed prior to launch. Other major use-testing procedures are gamma and delta testing. Gamma testing is the assessment of a product's use and safety concerns by other interested parties such as distributors, the media, and interest groups; delta testing is a periodic voluntary recall of a random sample of a product for a comprehensive performance analysis. When such a recall is made directly from customers, the company often offers new replacement products as an incentive. In some industries, delta testing is not new. Airlines, for example, are required by law to inspect regularly and to repair their planes after a set number of miles flown. Automobile companies routinely buy back a few of their own cars and those of their competitors from used-car dealers and car rental companies so that they can conduct a complete inspection.

Even before a product reaches the testing stage, designers can be taking steps that will make a recall easier. Products that have built-in traceability (typically, parts marked with individual serial numbers indicating the time and place of manufacture) and modularity (designs that facilitate replacement of components) will, in a recall situation, help managers diagnose and solve the problem quickly and cost-effectively.

Once a recall is issued, the product development team should focus on finding the cause of the problem and the best solution. On occasion, that team may be too close to the problem to assess it effectively. If necessary, an outside expert should be consulted to expedite the process and provide an impartial analysis of the problem. The product development team should also work with the recall response team to determine an appropriate adjustment offer to compensate the customer. More than any other group within the company, the product development team is aware of the effort and cost required to repair or replace the product in question.

After a recall, the product development team should conduct additional studies of the product defect with an eye to identifying any glitches in the development process that contributed to the problem. The team should study the science and technology behind the development process, reappraise its TQM process—especially the link between design and manufacturing—and identify additional opportunities for redesign (such as improvements in modularity) in anticipation of future problems.

Finally, the product development team should be involved in gathering customers' reactions to the product replacement, or at least be well informed of that feedback. Are customers satisfied with the new offering? Is it performing as expected? When possible, the product development team should conduct delta tests on the modified product.

COMMUNICATIONS

The communications function plays a central role in preparing an organization for recalls. In fact, the effectiveness of communication during and after a recall depends on prior communication—internally and externally—particularly for companies with products and services that span global markets. In the Perrier example, although the company was prompt in ordering a recall, poor communication damaged its brand image. *Customer communications can reinforce the company's image as a responsible organization.* Explanations of the source of the benzene differed: Perrier in the United States reported that the contamination was limited to North America; Perrier in the United Kingdom said that it did not know what had happened; in France, the company announced that the origin of the benzene was a cleaning fluid mistakenly used on the North American bottling line and that the water source was unaffected. Three days after *that* announcement, the company established that the problem was indeed located at the source; the contamination had been caused by a failure to replace charcoal filters that were used to screen out impurities.

As part of recall preparation and to aid people in communications, the manager with overall responsibility for recalls should identify major recall stakeholders (beyond immediate consumers). These might include distributors, dealers or retailers, financial institutions, employees, service centers, sales forces, and regulatory agencies. All those parties have a vested interest in how the company weathers a recall, and all should be kept abreast of the company's plans and actions (as appropriate) as the recall unfolds. Clearly it is important to build the organization's credibility in the eyes of those stakeholders in anticipation of the need for a recall. Many companies already have crisis-management communications plans that can address a variety of crises, whether they be labor relations issues or regulatory or criminal investigations. Recalls should be included in those plans. For companies that are in the process of developing crisis-management communications plans, a recall scenario might provide a suitable prototype issue.

During a recall, the response team should keep customers properly informed and persuade them to complete the necessary exchanges. Customer communications can reinforce the company's image as a responsible organization. Team members also should decide on and release appropriate messages to the media. For example, they might decide to preempt their current advertising with specially designed recall advertising. To carry out recall communications successfully, the recall response team should draw on the experience and expertise of people from public relations, advertising, and other sales and marketing resources.

After a recall, communications should focus on restoring and strengthening the company's reputation and the reputation of the product in question. The extent of that effort should be determined by the impact the recall has had on the stakeholders. We recommend, however, that as general practice, the communications members of the recall response team take at least some form of the following two actions.

Saturn's recall-related advertising campaign is a classic example of seizing opportunities to tell success stories.

- They should inform and reassure customers and other stakeholders, customizing the message to the various audiences. That action—which might take the form of letters, press releases, or advertising—may be conducted in tandem with the marketing efforts to relaunch the product.

- They should seize opportunities to tell success stories, using publicity, special advertising, or special promotions. Again, this effort should be handled jointly by the company's marketing and public affairs departments. Saturn's recall-related advertising campaign is a classic example.

Black & Decker Corporation's recall of its 1988 Spacemaker Plus coffeemaker provides a good example of a coordinated communications effort based on a reverse marketing plan. The problem first came to the company's attention in December 1988, when someone called the company's toll-free customer-service line to complain about a fire involving a Spacemaker Plus coffeemaker. At that time, more than 25,000 people in any of the 90 million households in the United States were believed to own the Black & Decker coffeemaker. In-house testing revealed within 48 hours that the unit was indeed faulty and could overheat and catch fire despite a device that was supposed to shut it off if it overheated. So Black & Decker decided to implement a recall, and, because of the life-threatening implications of the defect, the company also committed to a 100% return rate.

The company's first recall-communications efforts consisted of memos to retailers, distributors, sales associates, and all internal employees. It also publicized an 800 number to enable coffeemaker owners to get in touch. (Shipment of the coffeemaker had been stopped shortly after the company learned of the potential for fires.) Black & Decker also sent out letters to customers who had completed product registration cards for the coffeemaker, and it issued press releases detailing how customers could get replacement units or full refunds.

Despite this coordinated, if conventional, approach, less than 10% of the coffeemakers had been returned three weeks after the company's initial announcements. So Black & Decker decided to implement a direct-marketing effort and intensify its public relations program (using such tools as revised press releases, press kits, point-of-purchase materials, and trade press materials).

The direct-marketing approach used a database compiled from such sources as owner registration cards for other Spacemaker products and the list of contestants who had entered a competition in *Good Housekeeping* that had offered the coffeemaker as a prize. The data also included lists of consumers with profiles that indicated they might be likely customers. The company contacted those people by phone and registered mail, and by the end of January 1989, 64% of the defective coffeemakers had been returned.

Black & Decker intensified its efforts still further. For example, it identified 24 of the 80 largest cities in the United States as "underachievers" with low response rates, increased public relations efforts there, and also sent likely customers in those locales special direct-marketing materials. By the end of 1989, additional mailings and press releases had resulted in an unprecedented 92% return. What's more, Black & Decker's campaign created customer goodwill, as demonstrated by numerous favorable letters from customers after the recall and subsequently confirmed in broader market research.

(Note that in general, return rates run well below 100%. The NHTSA reports that recall return rates for automobiles vary from 15% to 70%. A Consumer Product Safety Commission study reported an average return or repair rate of 54.4% with considerable variance for a sample of 128 recalls between 1978 and 1983. Variations in returns can depend on such factors as the level of awareness among distributors and consumers, the cost-benefit trade-off perceived by consumers in complying, the time period between the end of distribution and the start of the recall if the product is no longer distributed, how easy it is to contact consumers, the size of retail inventory, and the convenience of the remedy. Taking such factors into consideration will help managers establish realistic goals.)

Logistics and information systems are the backbone of a smooth recall process.

LOGISTICS AND INFORMATION SYSTEMS

A company's logistics and information systems are the physical backbone of a smooth recall process. They support all recall efforts undertaken by the recall champion and the response team. And they must be flexible enough to absorb the shock of a recall without letting it disrupt regular operations. For example, the pipeline for products and parts may need to accommodate a two-way flow for a certain period of time while the company pulls in units to repair or replace even as it continues to release new or substitute models. To ensure that the systems will be able to handle the strain, the senior manager in charge of recalls might consider conducting a mock recall to test for product traceability and to establish whether existing distribution and information systems can get products back from customers efficiently.

The logistics and information systems also should have the ability to accept notification of product defects. For example, it is important to have a toll-free customer-service line operated by people who understand how to react and who know to whom they should report if they hear that a product is defective. Customer service personnel may need training to be sensitized to recalls. Notwithstanding the successful outcome of the Intuit case, the company's customer-service department did fail to grasp the significance of the first reports of the tax-software problem.

During a recall, the logistics and information systems should be able to trace any product that they have handled. That is, the systems should be able to isolate a product defect by batch, plant, process, or shift through the use of identifiers such as serial numbers. The logistics and information systems should also incorporate recall planning into management information systems, including databases, thereby maintaining product traceability records attached to customer files. Such a capability allows a company to monitor a recall's progress accurately and efficiently. In the Black & Decker coffeemaker recall, temporary workers were brought in to load the company's customer database with the names and addresses of 70,000 likely owners. Some 30 different types of letter, each including a postage-paid reply form, were prepared and mailed to the people on the lists. As a recall progresses, the ability to trace product ownership through customer files also helps ascertain if the correct product information— regarding specific defects and proposed solutions—is being passed along and utilized. In addition, it helps managers monitor return rates. With the help of the databases, managers can identify and get in touch with customers or distributors who have not responded.

After the recall, an assessment of logistics difficulties may provide valuable insights that will strengthen future distribution. Recall data also can facilitate a useful audit of the recall process. The logistics representative on the response team should maintain the recall logistics system for a time even after the recall is officially over, to collect stragglers. That person also might consider building a dedicated, ongoing, recall database to accumulate information to aid future recall decisions.

From Trouble, Opportunity

The potential consequences of a recall are clear. Recalls can shatter consumer confidence in a brand or company. They can disrupt channel and supplier relationships. They can make a company vulnerable to opportunistic competitors. They may invite regulatory interference. They may even cause an otherwise solid organization to become unstable.

But recall damage can be kept in check. And, in many cases, unavoidable recalls can be turned into opportunities with long-term favorable outcomes. Kenneth E.

Homa, formerly Black & Decker's vice president of marketing for household products, had this to say about the Spacemaker Plus recall:

"A recall is, in the final analysis, a costly distraction from normal business routines caused by a failure in internal development and operating processes. Accordingly, every effort is made to avoid recall situations by continually elevating quality standards and tightening process controls. But when the need arises, every possible effort is expended to execute a recall most effectively by acting quickly, setting heroic return goals, assigning strong people to the teams, refusing to quit until the task is complete, and recognizing the people who get the job done. Anything less could jeopardize the Black & Decker brand franchise and, unacceptably, put one of the company's key strategic assets at risk."

The recall-management framework we have presented is suggestive rather than definitive because recalls are different for each organization, each time. Senior managers need to assess their approach to recalls according to criteria of efficiency, effectiveness, and ethical consequences in order to establish their own framework for success. Ideally, a company will treat a recall as a part of its ongoing planning process so that not only is it prepared before one occurs, but it also recognizes the need for effective implementation when one does occur and can bring effective resolution along with value-added learning for the organization afterward.

Notes

1. Jim Carlton and Stephen K. Yoder, "Humble Pie: Intel to Replace Its Pentium Chips," *Wall Street Journal*, December 21, 1994.

2. Dean Foust, "Good Instincts at Intuit," *BusinessWeek,* March 27, 1995.

Originally published in September–October 1996
Reprint 96506

Right Away and All at Once:
How We Saved Continental

GREG BRENNEMAN

Executive Summary

IN 1993, WHEN GREG BRENNEMAN started working at Continental Airlines, it was the most dysfunctional company he had ever seen. It had been through two bankruptcies and ten presidents in ten years. There was next to no strategy. The company was burning through money. And employee morale couldn't get any worse.

Today Continental is flying high. It posted revenues of $7.2 billion and a net income of $385 million in 1997. It regularly ranks as one of the top five U.S. airlines for key performance measures such as dispatch reliability. And employee turnover has been drastically reduced.

What happened? In this first-person account, Brenneman, now Continental's president and COO, describes how he and the new team at Continental's helm transformed the company "right away and all at once." More specifically, he describes the five lessons he learned during this dramatic turnaround.

At the beginning, there was so much wrong with Continental that he felt as if any one misstep could bring the whole effort down. But in a time of crisis, when time is tight and money is tighter, you can't afford to mull over complex strategy. With Gordon Bethune, Continental's chairman and CEO, Brenneman devised the *Go Forward Plan,* a straightforward strategy focused on four key elements: understanding the market, increasing revenues, improving the product, and transforming the corporate culture.

He admits that the plan wasn't complicated—it was pure common sense. The tough part was getting it done. "Do it now!" became the rallying cry of the movement, and the power of momentum has carried Continental to success.

I WILL NEVER FORGET my first flight from Dallas to Houston on Continental Airlines. It was a hot, humid day in May 1993. At the time, I was a partner specializing in corporate turnarounds in Bain & Company's Dallas office. My goal that day was to sell Bain's consulting services to Continental's CEO and new owner, a leveraged buyout firm that had just rescued the airline from its second bankruptcy in nine years.

Although I was a frequent flier with literally millions of miles racked up on other airlines, I had always avoided Continental because of its reputation for lousy service. In fact, back in 1990, when we were deciding where to locate Bain's Texas office, we specifically chose Dallas instead of Houston so we could use American rather than Continental for our constant business travel.

Continental lived up—or perhaps I should say down—to my expectations that day in May. Because I was not a frequent flier on Continental, I was seated in the last row of an unattractive and dirty DC-9. The airplane's interior had seven different color schemes, which I later found out was not uncommon. After all, Continental was the product of mergers among seven airlines; when a seat needed to be replaced, the company used whatever was in stock. Worse, no one had hooked up the plane's air-conditioning. Departure time came and went, and people continued to trickle on board for another 40 minutes. I found this remarkable given that the flight time was only 36 minutes. There were no announcements about our delay, and none of the crew seemed particularly concerned.

Finally, probably to prevent a riot, the captain turned on the DC-9's auxiliary power unit. This cooled down the airplane all right, but it also caused condensation to build up on the inside roof of the aircraft. When we took off at last—50 minutes late—the accumulated condensation flowed like a waterfall along the top of the baggage bins to the back of the airplane. It came pouring out above the center seat in the last row of coach—directly onto my head. My best suit and I were soaked.

To make a long story short—and it was a long day—Bain got the job. I wasn't sure if I should celebrate or commiserate with my colleagues. My first assignment was to help Continental lower its maintenance costs and improve its dispatch reliability—in other words, figure out a way to fix planes that were breaking down when they needed to be flying. Drastic changes were made: within a year we had reduced the annual maintenance budget from $777 million to $495 million, and the airline jumped from worst to first in the industry in dispatch reliability. But the company was still sinking fast. By the fall of 1994, Continental had blown much of the $766 million in cash that it had when it emerged from bankruptcy in April 1993.

In my six-odd years of working on turnarounds at Bain, I had never seen a company as dysfunctional as Continental. There was next to no strategy in place. Managers were paralyzed by anxiety. The company had gone through ten presidents in ten years, so standard operating procedure was to do nothing while awaiting new management. The product, in a word, was terrible. And the company's results showed it. Continental ranked tenth out of the ten largest U.S. airlines in all key customer-service areas as measured by the Department of Transportation: on-time arrivals, baggage handling, customer complaints, and involuntary denied boardings. And the company hadn't posted a profit outside of bankruptcy since 1978.

But even with all these obstacles, Continental pulled out of its nosedive, just before it hit the ground, and it soared. (For more on Continental's performance, see the exhibit "Climbing Again.") How did the reversal of fortunes happen? Looking back, I can see we were guided by five operating principles. Probably none of them will knock your socks off. In fact, sometimes when I talk to people about the lessons the turnaround taught us, they say, "Well, Greg, those seem simple enough. Maybe things were a bit dicey while it was happening, but it sure doesn't sound like brain surgery."

And they are right: saving Continental wasn't brain surgery. The actions required to revive a moribund company usually aren't. In Continental's case, we simply needed to fly to places people wanted to go, when they wanted to go, in clean, attractive airplanes; get them there on time with their bags; and serve food at meal-times. The tough part—like in most turnarounds—was getting all that done fast, right away, and all at once.

Climbing Again

Continental Airlines has undergone a dramatic and profitable turnaround in the past several years.

Revenue

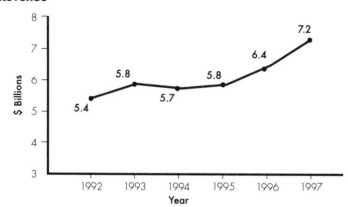

Net Income

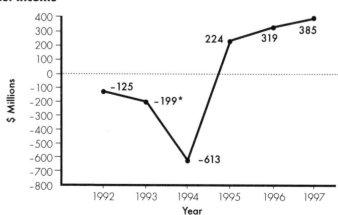

*This figure excludes bankruptcy-related items.

The fact is, you can't afford to think too much during a turnaround. Time is tight; money is tighter. If you sit around devising elegant and complex strategies and then try to execute them through a series of flawless decisions, you're doomed. We saved Continental because we acted and we never looked back. We didn't say to the patient—if you can call a dying company that—"Now, just hold on a while so we can run a lot of tests and then perhaps perform an extremely delicate 12-hour procedure." No, we just took out the scalpel and went to work. We gave the patient little or no anesthesia, and it hurt like hell. Then again, the patient is cured now, right?

One last thing before we get to the lessons. You will see the word *we* a lot as you read this article. In the broadest sense, *we* refers to my 40,000 coworkers at Continental. The airline could not have been saved if everyone in the company, and I mean everyone, had not pulled together. But in a narrower sense, *we* refers to myself and Gordon Bethune, Continental's chairman and CEO.

Gordon and I met in February 1994. I was still with Bain, in the midst of my first assignment for Continental. Gordon had just left a cushy job, or at least one where he could sleep soundly at night, at the Boeing Company to become president and COO of Continental. In me, Gordon found a frustrated consultant who bristled at the slow pace of change in most companies. In Gordon, I found an extraordinary leader who knew the airline business inside and out, and who managed the men and women of Continental with great heart. We hit it off from the start.

That was a good thing, because we were in a big mess together—bigger than either of us knew at first. Sure, we were able to fix some problems, such as an incredibly slow reservations system and a substandard customer-response policy. But those fixes were like trying to bail out the *Titanic* with a coffee can. Continental was losing an incredible amount of money and, more important, burning through cash at an astonishing rate. We were on our way to a third bankruptcy.

In October 1994, Continental's CEO resigned. That left Gordon nominally in charge, and he asked me to help. He moved into the CEO's office, and I moved into his old office. We had a week to put together a turn-around plan for Continental and develop a pitch to the board to name Gordon the CEO.

Throughout that week, Gordon and I held several dinner meetings—dubbed our "Last Suppers"—at his house. We knew a major ending was on the horizon—either the old Continental was going to be entirely reinvented or it was going to go bankrupt for an unprecedented third time and would probably be liquidated. Over several bottles of wine, we wrote down everything that was wrong with Continental. It was a very long list. We organized our solutions to those problems into a strategy that we called the *Go Forward Plan*. We named it that because we knew our history was not going to help us. Did you know that there are no rearview mirrors on an airplane? The runway behind is irrelevant.

Our Go Forward Plan had four cornerstones. *Fly to Win* was the market plan: we were going to build up our Houston, Newark, and Cleveland hubs, for instance, and expand our customer mix from backpacks and flip-flops to suits and briefcases. *Fund the Future* was the financial plan: we were going to gain liquidity by restructuring our balance sheet and selling off nonstrategic assets. *Make Reliability a Reality* was the product plan: we were going to transform the customer's experience with us. And finally, *Working Together* was the people plan: we were going to change Continental's culture to one of fun and action and restore employees' trust. It was my opinion then, and remains today, that every company should have a strategy that covers these four elements—market, financial, product, and people—whether it is in a severe crisis or not.

Gordon and I weren't totally convinced that Continental could be saved, even with our plan. But we had to try—40,000 jobs were at stake. It was scary. And for me, it was a defining moment. I was thinking, "Greg, this is one of those times in life when you step up to the plate or you chicken out." I had spent the last six years making recommendations that my clients sometimes took and sometimes ignored. I wanted to make things happen. It was going to take hard work, but that didn't worry me. I'm from a little farming town in Kansas where hard work is a way of life. I held a paying job when I was in third grade, and no one even blinked. In the summer of my junior year in high school, I mowed lawns from 6:30 a.m. until noon, delivered office furniture from noon until 6:00 p.m., and then baled and stacked hay until midnight. Frankly, I'd rather be working than not any day of the week.

Most important, even with all the work ahead, turning Continental around seemed like it was going to be fun. Grueling—without a doubt. Painful—certainly. Embarrassing—maybe, if we failed. But fun—yes. It's thrilling to lead people to do something no one thinks can be done. In fact, when we went before the board, we told them Continental could earn about $40 million in 1995. I know most of them thought we were on drugs. But who else was there volunteering to save Continental? The board approved the plan, and we were on our way.

Believe it or not, at this point I still wasn't on Continental's payroll. But both David Bonderman of Air Partners (the LBO firm that owned the airline) and Gordon were pushing me to join. They kept telling me I could be the only 33-year-old to run a $6 billion company. I kept telling them it was the world's worst $6 billion company. In spite of my reservations, I signed on. I truly believed the men and women of Continental could make the airline great again. We just had to get in there and do it.

File Your Flight Plan and Track Your Progress

The foundation of any successfully run business is a strategy everyone understands coupled with a few key measures that are routinely tracked. Now, strategic direction is always important, but I would make the case that it is particularly important during a turnaround. In crisis situations, managers usually have limited time and financial resources. If you have very little money to spend and you have to spend it very quickly, you had better have a clear idea of the most leveraged plan of action. Moreover, pressure and fear often make managers do erratic, inconsistent, even irrational things. Companies may veer from one "strategy" to another just to make payroll or keep a client. Continental was a case in point. When we took over, you probably couldn't find a single employee, even among senior management, who could tell you the company's strategy. There had been so many over the past decade that they'd stopped keeping track.

Oh sure, people paid lip service to strategy. Here's a classic example. When I first arrived at Continental as a consultant, 18% of the flights were cash negative. I knew the fastest way to make money was to stop doing things that lose it. I sat the scheduling team down and started asking questions. "Why are we going from Greensboro to Greenville six times a day when both customers who want to fly that route are on the first flight?"

"It's strategic," someone told me.

"When did it last make money?"

"It never did," was the reply.

"How strategic can that be?"

There was silence. I asked, "Does someone's boyfriend or girlfriend live there? Why don't we just charter you a Lear jet? It would be cheaper." That route, along with other cash-draining flights, was soon eliminated, and 7,000 employees were let go.

To put an end to Continental's strategic wandering, Gordon and I introduced the Go Forward Plan to our coworkers. It was our story and we were sticking to it (to borrow a line from a country-and-western song). The Go Forward Plan wasn't complex. It was pure common sense. We needed to stop flying 120-seat planes with only 30 passengers on them. We needed to get people to their destinations on time with their bags. We needed to start serving food when people were hungry. We needed to create an atmosphere where people liked coming to work. (For details of the strategy, see the exhibit "Continental's New Flight Plan.")

To implement the plan immediately and in its entirety, we sold it to our coworkers with energetic zeal. We knew that the two of us could not save Continental on our own. But if we could get every employee headed in the same direction, we had a chance. At the same time, we chose 15 or so key performance measures to track relentlessly and to compare against our competitors. We didn't pick randomly; we chose measures that could be verified by the Department of Transportation. Moreover, the measures had to be aligned with the Go Forward Plan. To monitor our performance in the marketplace, we decided to track our monthly load factor, revenue per available seat mile, and quarterly cost and

Continental's New Flight Plan

With little time and even less money to save the airline in 1994, Continental's leaders devised the *Go Forward Plan*, a four-part strategy focused on the fundamentals.

Fly to Win was the airline's marketplace plan; *Fund the Future* was the financial plan; *Make Reliability a Reality* was the formula to improve the product; and *Working Together* was the blueprint for improving the company's culture.

There was nothing complex about the Go Forward Plan: it was just a matter of logic and common sense. It remains the backbone of the company's strategy today.

Fly to Win

Focus on core assets: Stop scheduling flights that lose money. Take out cost as we take out capacity. Eliminate CALite. Build up Houston, Newark, and Cleveland hubs.

Expand customer mix from backpacks and flip-flops to suits and briefcases.

Revise marketing policies to enhance relationships with travel agents, corporations, and frequent fliers.

Goal
Increase revenues and deliver a profit.

Fund the Future

Track cash.

Restructure the balance sheet.

Restructure the fleet: Reduce the number of fleet types from 13 to 4. Match airplane size with market size. Eliminate above-market leases on airplanes.

Sell nonstrategic assets.

Goal
Secure liquidity.

Make Reliability a Reality

Perform in the top 50% of the industry on key DOT metrics: On-time performance Baggage mishandles Customer complaints Involuntary denied boardings

Improve image of fleet: Paint interiors and exteriors. Add phones. Offer first-class seats.

Improve aircraft cleanliness.

Improve food service.

Goal
Improve the product to become an airline of preference.

Working Together

Restore employee confidence in management: Offer on-time incentives. Establish a consistent and reliable flight schedule. Improve communication. Deliver a profit and introduce profit sharing.

Maintain peace among the work groups.

Establish a results-oriented culture: Let people do their jobs without interference. Treat one another with dignity and respect.

Goal
Build a new corporate culture.

profit margins. To monitor our product, we decided to track our monthly on-time performance, mishandled bags, customer complaints, and the rate of involuntary denied boardings. And to monitor the progress of our people plan, we decided to track turnover, sick leave, attrition, and on-the-job injuries.

Finally, and perhaps most important, to monitor our financial progress, we announced we were going to track cash. Let me tell you why. On Thanksgiving Day in 1994, I discovered that we were going to run out of cash on January 17, 1995—payday—and no one even knew it. I mean, no one had a clue. As you all know, cash is the lifeblood of any business. Without it, all your great plans to have a product you are proud of and people who like coming to work every day are meaningless. The buzzer will go off before you attempt the last shot, and you will lose.

You may be wondering why Continental's cash situation came as such a surprise. The reason tells you a lot about how people act when their companies are in a self-destructive mode. Some of the finance people had regularly been inflating our profit projections by plugging in overoptimistic revenue estimates. They felt pressured to do so, they said. In our business, revenue comes from credit card receipts. Naturally, our cash-flow forecasts always came in lower than projected because revenue (and thus, credit card receipts) was overstated. To this day, I can't understand why anyone would try to hide an impending cash shortage. Sure, it's bound to make the shareholders very unhappy, but hiding the fact that you are about to run out of money is like resetting the fuel gauge when you're low on gas. Will things suddenly look okay in the cockpit? Yes. Will you land short of your destination? You bet.

When I discovered Continental's real cash situation, I called Gordon. "I have some bad news for you," I told him. "Unless we restructure our obligations, we will not be able to make payroll in mid-January." While both our hearts were beating a million times an hour, we had a remarkably calm conversation. We could either declare bankruptcy or we could try to convince our creditors that the Go Forward Plan was going to work and then craft a very quiet restructuring. It had to be quiet because if the press caught on, the headlines would send more customers running, taking our revenues with them.

A couple of days later, I found myself in a room with our largest creditors. They represented approximately $3.5 billion of our $5 billion in debt and capitalized aircraft leases. I took them through the current situation, what we were doing to fix it, and the help we needed from them. They began ranting and raving. After a while, when it became apparent we were going nowhere, I got up to leave the room.

"Where are you going?" they shouted.

"I'm going home to watch TV," I answered.

"How can you drop all this on us and then leave?" they demanded.

"Do you know what the first step in problem solving is?" I asked. After a moment of dead silence, I continued, "The first step in problem solving is asking, Who has got the problem? As near as I can tell, if you take the share price times the number of shares outstanding, this entire company is worth $175 million and you are in hock for $3.5 billion. You run the company." Then I walked out.

I have never seen the team that managed a company into a crisis be able to get it back on track.

I'll never know what possessed me to say that. Maybe it was the 20-hour days I was working. Maybe it was the fact that I had seen a client of mine do largely the same thing during a real estate restructuring, to great effect. Maybe I was just fed up with the fact that everyone seemed to have a problem but no one had any solutions. But a few minutes later, the creditors came to my office and asked me to come back in. Things were much calmer. With the help of some talented financial experts, within a few weeks we had worked out a plan to restructure our debt. We made payroll on January 17 with the help of a $29 million wire transfer Gordon arranged from Boeing.

After that crisis was over, we knew we would never lose track of our cash again. It's all part of knowing our flight plan and monitoring our progress every mile of the way.

Clean House

I have never seen the team that managed a company into a crisis get it back on track. Oh, I'm sure it has happened some time in the history of business, but I can't believe it has happened very often. Instead, managers who have gotten a company into a mess are usually mired in a puddle of overbrained solutions. They can't see any way out either. In fact, they have many ways of saying, "If the solution were simple, we would have already thought of it." On top of that, they usually have trouble accepting responsibility for and reversing the poor decisions they made in the past. It's an ego thing. And there's one more problem with existing management teams sticking around for a turnaround. No one in the company trusts them anymore. They got us into this hole, the thinking goes, how are they going to have the sense to get us out of it?

Those are the main reasons we decided to clean house when we took over at Continental. But there were others. People want to be led, not managed, in a time of crisis. Members of Continental's existing management team were not up to this challenge. They were too busy trying to knock each other off. In fact, for 15 years, the way to get ahead at Continental was to torpedo someone and then take his or her job.

Gordon and I were determined to present a united front. No one was going to come between us; if they tried, they were out. I will always remember my first meeting with all the officers at Continental. Gordon started the meeting by saying, "Greg is going to take you through our plan to get this company back on track. I want you to listen to what he has to say, and when he tells you to do something, you assume it is coming from me, and do it."

In the span of a couple of months, we replaced 50 of our 61 officers with about 20 individuals. We were cutting bureaucracy and costs but also putting important stuff—like the right culture—back in. All new hires had to have three qualities. First, they had to pass what we called the "raw IQ test"—there is no substitute for smarts. Second, they had to be driven to get things done. Finally, they had to be team players, willing to treat everyone with dignity and respect in an extremely collaborative environment.

Speaking of dignity and respect, cleaning house needn't be a brutal or humiliating experience. Every turnaround involves creating a new culture. If you fire people inhumanely, you'll be left with a bunch of employees who don't trust the company or their coworkers. We needed to create a culture at Continental where people liked coming to work. We couldn't afford to have people hoarding ideas or sapping enthusiasm as we built our new organization. So when we let people go, we went out of our way to be fair by honoring their contracts and letting them resign with dignity.

We are often asked how we got such great people in the span of only a couple of months, especially at a company that appeared to be going down the tubes. The answer is, we started by hiring people we knew, many of whom were our friends. That expedited the process of screening candidates and greatly reduced our hiring mistakes. Some of these managers had spent their careers in the airline business and some hadn't worked a day at an airline. One of our techniques was to find people who were in a number two position in their current job and ask them to join Continental in the number one spot. For instance, we'd ask the number two person in pricing at another airline to come run our pricing department. We promised them full control of their domains.

When you are bleeding cash, it's hard to think of anything but tourniquets. But Continental had been cutting costs in ways that sabotaged its products.

And we sold Continental as if it were already a winner. At the time, our stock was trading at about $7, but I told people we wanted to hire that we were going to drive it up to $80 or higher. We offered them options along the way, so if the shareholders won, they would win. Most of them thought I was nuts, but as one of them later told me, "I figured if you were even half right, I was still going to be worth a lot of money." (And, in fact, the turnaround created many millionaires.)

It's important to point out that we didn't just clean house on the top floor of Continental. We went through the entire organization—from the highest supervisors to the baggage handlers. Many companies in crisis mode will change the CEO or president and leave it at that. In my opinion, that approach is like changing only the lead husky on a sled-dog team. Four dogs back, the look and smell stays the same. When you want real change, you can't do it partway. You have to do it fast, right away, and all at once.

Think "Money in," Not "Money out"

Every turnaround involves cost reduction, and Continental was no exception. Most companies that are in trouble, however, tend to develop a myopic focus on cost. They forget to ask simple questions like, Do we have a product people want to buy? Will our distributors sell our product? and, Are we taking care of our best customers? In short, they forget to think about money in, or good old revenues.

Of course, when you are bleeding cash, it's hard to think about anything but tourniquets. But Continental had been cutting costs in ways that sabotaged its product. For instance, in the early 1990s, pilots earned bonuses if the fuel burn rate on their airplanes fell below a specified amount. The program did decrease fuel costs, but it motivated many pilots to skimp on air-conditioning. (Indeed, the program may have been the reason behind my first "refreshing" experience with Continental.) It also motivated them to fly more slowly. That made our customers late and angry and ruined the lives of our employees who had to work overtime because of tardy arrivals. It also forced the airline to pay more to accommodate customers who had to take other airlines because of missed connections.

Perhaps the ultimate manifestation of Continental's low-cost approach was CALite, the company's doomed low-cost airline-within-an-airline. For CALite, Continental removed all first-class seats in some airplanes. That lowered the cost per seat mile by adding more seats, but it alienated Continental's best business customers and often resulted in an all-coach airplane on long flights when airplanes were swapped during adverse weather conditions. CALite eliminated all food on its flights, and it also eliminated travel agent commissions and corporate discounts, which infuriated some very important customers.

All told, after 15 years of a low-cost approach, Continental had created what I call a *doom loop*. By focusing only on costs, the airline had created a product no one wanted to buy. Many customers, particularly business customers with a choice, selected other airlines, reducing revenues enough to create huge losses. Those losses made it impossible to borrow money at reasonable rates. Management then had to borrow from "pawn shops" to keep the company afloat, which increased interest expenses. In order to make up for these increased expenses, management cut costs further. Since the costs of the aircraft and fuel were fixed, and costs such as food had already been cut, the only way to reduce costs was to take back wages from employees. That ticked them off (to put it in language this publication will permit), which caused further reductions in service. As a result, more customers left, revenues continued to drop, and costs had to be cut more and more.

You might think the first step in breaking the doom loop is to fix the product, but that's actually the second step. The first is to beg forgiveness from all the customers you have wronged. Sure, you can skip this step, but you'll miss out on the goodwill it fosters and the relationships it spawns. Confession is good for everyone's soul, and often for the pocketbook as well.

Our forgiveness campaign had a couple of parts. First, we divided the angry letters from customers among our officers—executives through the rank of vice president—and started making phone calls. Our goal was not only to apologize but also to explain what we were doing to fix the company. Gordon and I each took our share of the letters. It was a humbling experience. The calls would often last half an hour or more. People were incredibly frustrated and wanted to let us know how badly they had been treated. By the end of the call, however, they were usually appreciative that an officer of the company had taken the time to seek them out.

We also assigned one city in our system to each officer and asked them to go through the same process of apologizing to travel agents and corporate customers. Gordon and I took the largest of those accounts. Again, we heard our share of shouting—there was a lot of venom out there. But at the same time, people couldn't believe that we were coming around to say we were sorry and to thank them for their business. I never denied that Continental had been a terrible airline. In fact, I usually agreed with everything they said. But I also wanted them to know that a new beginning was under way.

The third step in breaking the doom loop was to cut our advertising budget in half. It is offensive and insulting to customers to advertise a product that they know is crummy. Until the time came when we could offer them something great, I didn't want to promote a product that we couldn't deliver. So advertising less—lying less—was another way of saying we were sorry.

Begging for forgiveness can be unpleasant, that's for sure. But it's indispensable if you want to break the doom loop. Only after that has begun can you move on to making money—the subject of the next principle.

Ask the Customer in Seat 9C the Right Question

Deciding to focus more on customers' desires rather than on cutting costs is actually the easy part. The hard part is figuring out how to improve the customer's experience so that revenues increase faster than costs. Any first-year marketing student can tell you that to make more money, you have to listen to your best, most lucrative customers. In our case, that meant listening to the customers in seat 9C, the business travelers who book the aisle seats near the front of the plane. They pay full fare, and they travel a lot.

But we knew we couldn't listen to everything the customers in seat 9C had to say. If you ask customers what they really want, they will write you an epistle a foot thick. If you ask them what they want *and will pay extra for,* you will get a single sheet of paper with requests. That's where our focus was, and it's a good rule for any turnaround.

Relying mostly on our own experience as business travelers, we knew that the customer in seat 9C would pay extra for a few things: airplanes and terminals that are safe, comfortable, and attractive; on-time flights and reliable baggage handling; and good food at mealtimes. With the exception of safety, where Continental had always had a strong record, we were failing miserably on all counts.

We went to work at full speed. We asked the maintenance department to paint the exterior of every airplane the same and to match all the interiors. We also ordered new carpeting for all the airport terminals, and we launched a campaign to "retire the meatball"—that is, replace the old Continental logo, which was round, red, and ugly, with a blue globe with gold lettering. And we wanted it all done in six months.

The maintenance department was not amused. "Greg," I was told, "You have just proven you don't know anything about the airline business. You're asking for a four-year project." My response: "If you can't get it done, we'll find someone who will." Lo and behold, within six months, every plane was painted the same color inside and out, and all of the terminals had new carpeting. Our maintenance team worked their fannies off, and Continental's handsome new image was everywhere. Chalk one up for the power of persuasion.

Our customers loved Continental's new look. Who wouldn't after flying on the old Continental? In March 1995, I boarded a 737-100, which at 27 years was the oldest airplane in our fleet. The gentleman sitting next to me looked at me and said, "Isn't it great that Continental is getting all these new airplanes?" I just smiled.

The new image had an even bigger impact on our employees. They could see senior management finally taking the actions they knew had been needed for years. They could come to work in airports and on airplanes that looked clean and new. One of our MD-80 captains called me and said, "Greg, I knew we would be a good airline again once our airplanes were the same color."

We also started an aircraft appearance department to make sure our airplanes would continue to look great day after day. We learned that in one of the early cost-reduction programs, management had decided to clean the airplanes less frequently and to have the pilots clean their own cockpits. We quickly set up a cleaning schedule that tripled the number of times the airplanes are cleaned, cockpits included.

As for improving reliability, we had to get two sets of folks talking to each other: those that wrote the flight schedules and those that ran the flight and airport operations. In the past, the scheduling department had simply written a flight schedule and given it to operations, often only days before they were to fly it, because it was "confidential." As a result, the operating departments were frequently stuck with a schedule they had no hope of following: they had mechanics, parts, and crews in the wrong locations. Very quickly, we required the scheduling and operating departments to review and sign off on the flight schedules before they were loaded to be flown. Presto, now people were in control of their own destiny, and the finger-pointing stopped.

Once Continental had a flight schedule that could be operated on time, we made an offer to our employees. For every month we finished in the top five out of ten airlines in on-time performance as measured by the DOT, we would give each employee $65. Incentives were now aligned; when the customers won, the employees did, too. Within months, we were regularly finishing first.

The offer sounds pretty bold for a company almost in bankruptcy, doesn't it? Truth is, the on-time incentive program is self-funding. When we made the offer, we were paying about $6 million per month to reaccommodate our customers on our competitors' flights. We were taking in approximately $750,000 per month. Since reaccommodation expenses showed up in a contrarevenue account rather than as a cost on the general ledger, they escaped the eyes of the cost reduction program. As an

on-time airline, we pay out only $750,000 in reaccommo-
dation expenses while taking in $4 million. Our balance
of payments has changed by $8 million to $9 million per
month. The on-time bonus costs only $3 million per
month.

We also immediately started fixing our idiotic food
policy. I don't know about you, but to me, a two-hour
flight that leaves at 7:00 A.M. (after I have gotten up at
5:00 A.M. to get to the airport and haven't eaten breakfast) is a lot different from a two-hour flight at 2:00 P.M.,
which falls after lunch but before dinner. Customers told
us they wanted and would pay for breakfast at 7:00 A.M.
They may want food at 2:00 P.M., but they won't pay for
it. We changed our meal service with an eye toward what
our competitors were doing. Now our service reflects
time of day, length of haul, and class of service.

In addition to changing *when* we served food, we
also changed the food itself. Gone are the days when
Continental put the meat, potato, and vegetable in a
little ceramic dish and heated it until they all tasted the
same. Nowadays, Gordon
and I personally select the
food we serve on our
planes, and we test it ourselves every three months.
You will find items like
fresh pasta, soup and
sandwiches, and freshly baked cinnamon rolls in first
class, and Subway sandwiches and jelly beans in
coach. We try to give everyone some brand quality with
gourmet coffees and microbrewery beers. We're not
trying to be a four-star restaurant, just an airline
that gives its customers something they'd be happy to
pay for.

*The employees were
going to be liberated—to be
able to do right by the
customer and to have fun
at work.*

And that's the whole point of asking the customer in seat 9C the right question. In a turnaround situation—or any business situation, for that matter—you can't afford to ask anything else.

Let the Inmates Run the Asylum

I'm not going to tell you that all the employees at Continental are "empowered." We fly airplanes, after all. When people's lives are at stake, certain rules and procedures are not open to interpretation or reinvention on a daily basis. And when you are an airline in a do-or-die situation, you don't exactly let your employees sort out strategy. It would take too long, and it's no way to act when strong leadership is imperative.

But within the parameters set for safety and those we set with the Go Forward Plan, we decided that at the new Continental, the employees were going to be liberated—to be able to do the right thing by the customer and to have fun at work.

Now, fun at work isn't about dancing on the tarmac. In fact, I think the word *fun* scares a lot of executives. They picture productivity plummeting, and profits along with it. But I would argue that people have fun at work when they are engaged, when their opinions are respected. People are happy when they feel they are making a difference.

When I arrived at Continental, it was a mean and lousy place to work. For years, different groups of employees had been pitted against one another in the effort to drive down labor costs. Management's implicit communication policy had been, Don't tell anybody anything unless absolutely required. As a result, most employees learned of the company's activities, plans, and performance through the press. Talk about sending a message about who matters and who doesn't.

On top of that, employees had no place to go with ideas or questions. There were forms for employees' suggestions on how to improve the operations, but the suggestions disappeared into a black hole. Add to that the fact that corporate headquarters was locked up like Fort Knox: the president's secretary had a buzzer under her desk that she could use to summon the police.

Needless to say, morale was terrible. A couple of weeks after I arrived, I was walking the ramp in Houston saying hello to our mechanics and baggage handlers, and helping to throw a bag or two, when I noticed that almost all the employees had torn the Continental logos from their shirts. When I asked one mechanic why he had done this, he explained, "When I go to Wal-Mart tonight, I don't want anyone to know that I work for Continental." His response still sends chills down my spine.

Now, how to create a new culture is the topic of hundreds, if not thousands, of books and articles. But Gordon and I didn't bother with them. We agreed that a healthy culture is simply a function of several factors, namely: honesty, trust, dignity, and respect. They all go together; they reinforce one another. When they are constants in a business, people become engaged in their work. They care; they talk; they laugh. And then fun happens pretty naturally. But honesty and the rest don't just sprout up like weeds in a cornfield, especially when there has been a long drought. In a turnaround situation, people are tense and suspicious for good reason. They've been lied to. They've seen their friends get fired. They fear they will be next.

So cultivating honesty, trust, dignity, and respect becomes the job of the leaders. It may even be their most important job; Gordon and I certainly considered it our top priority. That's why when we took over, we started talking with employees at every opportunity. We got out there in the airports and on the planes. We loaded bags; we stood alongside the agents at ticket counters. We just talked at every opportunity about our plans for the airline and how we were going to accomplish them. In general, our communication policy changed from, Don't tell anybody anything unless absolutely required, to Tell everybody everything.

We also told our employees we believed in them. They knew how to treat customers right, and we moved quickly to let them do just that. In the past, any time an employee provided a benefit for a customer that was considered unacceptable, the bankers and lawyers running Continental would write a rule documenting the proper action. Over the years, these rules were accumulated into a book about nine inches thick known as the Thou Shalt Not book. Employees couldn't possibly know the entire contents of the book. When in doubt, everyone knew it was advised just to let the customers fend for themselves. In early 1995, we took the Thou Shalt Not book to a company parking lot. We got a 55-gallon drum, tossed the book inside, and poured gasoline all over it. In front of a crowd of employees, we lit a match to it. Our message was this: Continental is your company to make great. Go do it—now.

Because it is critical to get everyone working together, we aligned employees' compensation with the company's objectives. The on-time bonus I mentioned earlier made it clear that our employees would win when our customers did. We also put in several programs to ensure that our coworkers would win when our investors did. For most of our employees, one incentive is profit sharing. Our workers receive 15% of Continental's profits—which has worked out to be approximately 7% of their pay over the last two years. We have a great time riding in Brink's trucks distributing profit-sharing checks every Valentine's Day.

To involve our employees even more in the turnaround, we put up 650 bulletin boards throughout the system. These boards contain everything an employee needs to know about the company, from a daily news update to Continental's operating results over the last 24 hours. In addition, Gordon records a voice mail each Friday that summarizes the activities of the week. Every month, Gordon and I hold an open house where employees can ask us questions, and we publish a newspaper describing what's happening in the company. Every quarter, we send a *Continental Quarterly* magazine to employees' homes, and twice a year we do the same with a state-of-the-company video and recent press clippings. The video is produced for our semiannual employee meetings, when we travel to nine locations to update everyone on our progress. By the way, sending select material to the home is one of the smartest things you can do. The support you get from each employee's family when they become part of the team is incredible. Finally, each corporate officer is assigned a city on the system. It is his or her responsibility to visit the city once per quarter to update employees, get their feedback, and fix their problems.

Of course, we'd be fools if all we did was talk *at* our employees. We listen, too. We set up a toll-free hotline that operates around the clock to handle employees' suggestions. Pilots, flight attendants, mechanics, and gate agents manage the hotline. They are required to research each suggestion and get back to the employee within 48 hours with one of three responses: we fixed it; we are not going to fix it, and here is why; or, we need to study it a little more, and we will get back to you by such and such date. We have taken more than 200 calls per week in the three years the hotline has been open.

We don't implement all of the suggestions—I'd say about one in ten is implemented—but we take each one seriously. A group of baggage handlers came to me a little more than a year ago and asked if we could tag the bags of our best customers "priority" and deliver them first off the baggage belt. It sounded like a great idea, but I was worried we would raise expectations and then not be able to deliver. They explained that the process was easy: as you pull the bags off the airplane, the ones marked priority go in the first baggage cart, which is the first to be unloaded. Priority bags are a big hit. The program didn't cost anything, but it added value to the customer. Today the plan is in place across our entire system.

The kind of talking and listening I've described goes a long way toward creating an atmosphere of honesty, trust, dignity, and respect. But to go the full distance, we knew that we would also have to communicate openly when the message was tough. Let me tell you, for instance, about the day I had to shut down our operations in Greensboro, North Carolina.

The historical norm for delivering bad news at Continental was for a senior manager to dump the news in the local airport manager's lap and then hide in our corporate office building. But I decided to go to Greensboro myself, make the announcement to the employees, and take my punches publicly.

When I arrived the night before the meeting, I found several messages waiting for me from the head of our pilots' union. He wanted to meet for breakfast the next morning, and I quickly agreed. When we met, he said that the Greensboro pilots were not angry that we were closing the airport—they could see that there were no customers on the flights. But they did not feel that the compensation package was fair. I said I was surprised; we had just finished negotiating the first pilots' contract in 12 years, and it had been ratified by a large margin. Moreover, I had taken the financial relocation package called for in the contract and doubled it. I then offered it to all employees, not just pilots. Not mollified, the union president asked me to come to a meeting the pilots were having before my meeting with the entire airport staff.

That meeting was hostile, to put it mildly. But it would have been dishonest to back down or to fudge a reaction of sympathy I did not feel. I believed the pilots were getting a fair deal, and I said so. About an hour later, I met with the rest of the employees and their families—about 600 people in all. Along with explaining the details of the closing and relocation plans, I also shared with them my vision for Continental and how far we had come. I then opened the floor to questions and answers.

For about five minutes, employees expressed appreciation that I had personally come to give them the news and had developed a financial package to meet their needs. But then the pilots walked in—in full uniform—with their families. They surrounded the room and refused to sit down. A pilot came to the microphone to express how incompetent he felt management was and how Continental was once again making the wrong decision. The rest of the pilots applauded.

Do you know what happened? The rest of the employees, led by a baggage handler who was also being relocated, stood up and defended me, one after another, for 20 minutes. They told the pilots that they should feel lucky that Continental finally had a senior management team that treated them with enough respect to deliver the bad news—as well as a good relocation package—in person. I left to a standing ovation.

Closing Greensboro was one of the toughest days of my life. It is a heavy responsibility to make decisions that affect the lives of so many coworkers. But it was a tough and emotional time for everyone. The pilots weren't bad folks; in fact, many of them are good friends of mine now. They were just frustrated with 15 years of poor decisions and were taking it out on me—like blaming your third wife for all of your problems with the first two. So I tell this story not to vilify them but to demonstrate the kind of trust that starts to emerge when a company's leaders neither hide nor mince words in bad times. It's easy to make everyone happy when things are going well. But real trust is a 365-days-a-year commitment.

Continental is a fun place to work today. Lots of statistics prove that fact, such as the huge reductions in turnover, sick leave, on-the-job injuries, and worker's compensation claims. But my favorite measure is the sale of Continental logo merchandise at our company stores. The same employees who used to tear the patches from their shirts so no one would know they worked at Continental have increased their purchases of hats, caps, T-shirts, and the like for themselves and their friends by more than 400%.

There was so much wrong with Continental that I felt as if one little misstep could have brought us down.

That's the kind of thing that happens when you let the inmates run the asylum. You may feel as if you've lost a bit of your authority and control over every last detail—because you have—but that's okay. You can't run a company from the executive suite of an office building anyway. When the employees are happy, everyone is happy—from the customers to the shareholders.

The Power of Momentum

Sometimes people ask me, "Did anything about the turnaround surprise you?" My answer is, "The fact that it didn't fail."

That's an exaggeration, because as I've said, I had enormous faith in my coworkers at Continental and the powerful logic of the Go Forward Plan. But at the beginning of the turnaround, there was so much wrong with the company—so many parts of it to fix—I really felt as if one little misstep could have brought us down. A single creditor could have blocked our restructuring. The economy could have been in a downswing. The pilots could have rejected their contract. We were working hard, yes—but we had great luck, too.

When I look back now, I realize the biggest factor in our favor was momentum. The rallying cry of our turnaround was, "Do it fast, do it right away, do it all at once. Do it now!" We lit a fire of urgency beneath Continental; we rotated quickly and picked up speed as we climbed to 41,000 feet. Pretty soon, we were unstoppable. What a ride it has been. Of course, the ride isn't over. We have big plans for Continental and mustn't lose our momentum. Even though the turnaround is over, we won't forget the lessons we learned from it. In fact, we're putting them to practice every day.

Pulling out of a Nosedive: Five Turnaround Lessons

File your flight plan and track your progress.

Strategic direction is never more crucial than during a

crisis. Leaders must find the most leveraged plan of action, stick with it, and continually monitor the company's performance against it.

Clean house.

The same team that leads a company into a crisis is rarely able to get it back on track. The hard news about a turnaround is that you have no choice but to sweep out the old to make way for the new.

Think "money in," not "money out."

Companies that are headed for disaster try to cut costs, but that can sabotage the product, which lowers revenues more. Break the *doom loop* by apologizing for your mistakes and focus on delivering a better product.

Ask the customer in seat 9C the right question.

There is a huge gap between what customers want and what they are willing to pay for. Make sure you know the difference.

Let the inmates run the asylum.

Strong leadership, firm parameters, and clear direction are necessary in a turnaround situation, but the workplace needn't be repressive. In fact, if employees aren't having fun at work—that is, if they aren't engaged in the process and treated with respect—your turnaround will not succeed.

Originally published in September–October 1998
Reprint 98503

Media Policy—What Media Policy?

SANDI SONNENFELD

Executive Summary

EVERY YEAR SINCE 1982, Naturewise Apparel has donated $400,000 to charity through its Corporate Giving Fund. This year, Dana Osborne, founder and CEO of the children's clothing manufacturer, decided to allow each of the company's regional divisions to decide for itself where the money should go. Her goal was to include all employees in the program and to pay back the various local communities that support the company.

Dana's good intentions backfired, however, when an abortion clinic in Illinois was bombed and the bomber claimed affiliation with a radically pro-life group called TermRights. Naturewise's Midwest division had inadvertently provided donations to TermRights through a nonprofit umbrella corporation called CHICARE. To make matters worse for Naturewise—which has consistently supported environmental and antiviolence programs—the local TV station and the regional paper reported accounts of the incident in which they accused the company of condoning the violent action and of knowingly funding TermRights. When the TV station and the paper had called the Midwest division, all the head of corporate communications would say was, "No comment."

As the head of the division offered her resignation and Naturewise's communications manager suggested issuing a press release, Dana's assistant interrupted them to say that a reporter from a major city paper was on the phone and wanted to talk to Dana.

How should Dana handle the media? Should she take this call? Should she continue to go with "no comment"? Should she issue a formal press release? If so, what should its message be?

Five experts consider this fictitious scenario and give advice on forming an effective media policy.

DANA OSBORNE, founder and CEO of Naturewise Apparel, pulled her bright red Saturn into a parking space near the entrance to her company's headquarters in Seattle. She was eager to get to her office. The company was in negotiations to expand overseas, and Dana was expecting to hear from a potential joint-venture partner in Antwerp. The previous round of talks had gone well: managers of the Belgian enterprise had seemed enthusiastic about launching the Naturewise line of chemical-free natural-fiber children's wear. Today she could get the go-ahead.

She entered the building and rode the elevator to the eighth floor. As the doors opened, she could see Bob Hewitt, her communications manager, and Janet Steiner, the head of the Midwest division, waiting for her just inside the glass doors of her outer office.

Dana looked at her watch. What time was it in Belgium, anyway? And how come Janet was there?

Bob met Dana at the door. "We've got a problem," he said. "It has to do with the company's corporate giving fund."

Every year since 1982, when Naturewise had gone public, the company had donated $400,000 to charity. The program had always been administered by corporate headquarters, and the recipients had always been major national or worldwide relief organizations. This year, in an effort to include all employees in the program, Dana and her senior managers had agreed to allow each regional division to decide for itself where the money should go.

Dana motioned Bob and Janet into her private conference room.

"Okay, tell me."

Bob spoke slowly. "Our decision to make our giving program more focused is backfiring on us in a big way. You know we thought of this regional plan as a good public relations move—a way of paying back the various communities that support us—"

"We don't give to charities because it makes for good copy," Dana interrupted. "We do it because it's the right thing to do."

"I know, Dana. But we have a PR problem now. Janet's division gave its funds to a nonprofit umbrella corporation called CHICARE, which supports 140 social service organizations in Chicago and the Midwest. Unfortunately, one of those organizations happens to be TermRights, a radically pro-life group."

Dana looked over at Janet, who closed her eyes.

Bob continued. "Yesterday there was a bombing at an abortion clinic in Joliet, Illinois. And you can just guess which organization the bomber claims affiliation with."

"Was anybody hurt?" Dana asked.

Bob shook his head. "No. But last night a local TV news station aired a story announcing that Naturewise Apparel obviously condoned the action because we provide financial support to TermRights through CHICARE. They called the corporate communications office at the Midwest division, but Marc Russo there just gave them a 'no comment.' He did the same with the local paper, the *Will County Mirror*. The story came out this morning. I have a copy of it right here." (See "Kids' Store Funded Clinic Bombers" at the end of this article.)

Bob put the news clipping in front of Dana. She read it over quickly, dismayed at the accusatory tone of the piece, and handed it back to Bob.

"I hate that this happened," she said. "I would love to see this bomber go to jail forever. But the bottom line is that we didn't know the money was going to this particular group, did we?" She looked at Janet. "Clearly, we were remiss in not checking into CHICARE more

"Steven Randall of the **Chicago Daily Bulletin** *is on the line. He says he'll hold. What should I tell him?"*

carefully. But it is CHICARE that ultimately decides whom to fund and where the money goes, not us. We never expected our money to go to such an organization. We didn't want it to. We didn't know."

The room was silent. Dana could feel her stomach beginning to knot.

Then Janet spoke. "I should have researched CHICARE more thoroughly. It gives to so many worthy causes— AIDS research, environmental cleanups, shelters for the homeless, adult-literacy programs. It just never occurred to me that we'd run into a problem like this."

Inwardly, Dana cursed both Janet and the Midwest division for wreaking such havoc on the company. But she also knew that Janet wasn't a careless person. Hers was the top grossing division in the company.

"I know that if this gets much worse, you'll probably ask for my resignation," Janet continued. "I could make a statement to the papers that I did this on my own—that headquarters didn't know anything about it. After all, it's the truth."

"We should consider that," Bob cut in, surprised at the severity of his own response.

"No. That's not a reasonable solution," Dana said. "It wouldn't solve anything. Abortion is an emotional topic. Some of our customers are pro-choice; some are pro-life. And even if Janet resigned, rumors would circulate that we put pressure on her to do so. That could make things even worse."

"We're going in circles," Bob said. "We're going to need to make some kind of statement to the press—unless you think we should continue to go with 'no comment.'"

A knock at the door made them all look up. It was Caroline Gelston, Dana's administrative assistant. "Dana, I'm sorry to interrupt," Caroline said, "but Steven Randall of the *Chicago Daily Bulletin* is on the line. I said you weren't available, but he said he'd hold until you were. What should I tell him?"

How should Dana deal with the press?

Five experts discuss the components of an effective media policy.

MIKE WOODS *is a senior editor at Los Angeles-based* Investor's Business Daily.

Dana must take the call from the *Chicago Daily Bulletin*, but she doesn't have to answer any questions about the bombing.

Instead, Dana should tell the reporter that she would welcome questions about Naturewise's operation, including the company's overseas venture, but that inquiries about the bombing incident are being handled by Janet Steiner. With a bit of luck, the reporter will back off if Dana downplays the story's importance. But if he does drop a dime on Janet, Dana has at least bought a little time to come up with a better response than "no comment."

The last thing Dana should do is try to field questions about the incident herself or follow Bob's advice and issue a formal press release. Responding to an unfounded story only gives it credibility. The company has done nothing wrong.

As soon as Dana gets the reporter off the phone, she must put her company on the offensive by setting up a line of defense. While it's doubtful that any credible news organization would write a follow-up story on such flimsy evidence, Dana and her crew must prepare for the worst. For example, if reporters from the Associated Press, Bloomberg, or Dow Jones get wind of the story and call the company, the news may reach the investment world. That could result in some temporary pressure on the stock, which will upset faithful institutional investors and may prompt lawsuits by shareholders. Naturewise needs to be ready for that possibility.

First, Dana should ask Bob to compile a list of all the charities Naturewise supports. The list should include how long the company has supported those charities and how much money it has contributed over the years. It should also note whether the company has ever with-drawn support of a charity and, if so, why. Has Nature-wise contributed to more charities since enacting the regional program? If so, how many?

While he's at it, Bob should find out which other com-panies in the region give to charities. Many established organizations give to groups like the United Way, the Boy Scouts, and the Red Cross. Other large charities may channel their funds to groups with certain political agen-das. Is every organization that supports such an umbrella charity guilty if one of the charity's groups commits a felony?

Meanwhile, Dana should have Janet call CHICARE. Naturewise needs to know which other companies sup-port the organization, how long CHICARE has been in business, and whether this type of incident has ever hap-pened before. Is CHICARE planning to make a state-ment? If so, what is its position? Dana should keep in mind that CHICARE supports 140 organizations. Nature-wise gave it $150,000 this year. That's a little more than $1,000 per group—hardly the level of funding that could rationally be considered "support money."

If press attention from outside the region increases, that research will give Janet—now the designated spokesperson—something to talk about. She could explain, for example, that CHICARE is one of however many charities Naturewise supported this year. The oth-ers are the United Way, the Boy Scouts, the Red Cross, and so on. CHICARE, which funds 140 social service groups, is supported by x other companies doing busi-ness in the Chicago area. Janet could point out that Naturewise expanded its charitable-giving program this year in an effort to fund services in the regions in which it operates. The company's management decided that because employees help generate the profits, they should have a direct say in where the funds are distributed.

Putting Naturewise's charity program in perspective like that will probably prevent any more shoot-first, aim-later news stories. It may also educate the local press. Naturewise might also consider accusing both the local newspaper and television station of being antibusiness. Nowadays, an "I'm a victim" defense is a sound strategy that may turn a potentially damaging story into a positive event.

If, and *only* if, the company is flooded with calls from the media, Dana should consider issuing a press release to try to put the incident in perspective. She will have to take the pulse of the situation for the next few days and make decisions as events unfold.

Once she has set the immediate research projects in motion, Dana should call the company's lawyers to discuss what position Naturewise should take in response to the local coverage. My hunch is that the lawyers will say that the stories were defamatory and that the company may be able to prove that the coverage unfairly damaged its reputation.

If Dana doesn't get tough now, the local media may take another swing.

Armed with that information, Dana must call the editor of the *Will County Mirror* and the producer at the local TV station. She must be firm and clear about her intentions. She must explain the company's charity program and say that Naturewise is considering filing a lawsuit unless retractions are aired and published. Furthermore, she should say that she is writing a letter to the producer and the editor and request that it be read and published.

Too many companies worry that trying to set the record straight will only anger the press and encourage further slanted reports. In the long run, that kind of reticence doesn't pay. Judging from the coverage of this incident, Naturewise and the local media haven't seen eye to eye in the past, but now isn't the time to mend fences. If Dana doesn't get tough now, the TV station and the paper may take another swing.

I doubt, however, that they are preparing for another attack. More likely, the reporters and editors involved in the first round are having their own problems right now. My guess is that the publisher of the *Will County Mirror* is pretty upset with the editor and the reporter responsible for the original story. The tension level at the TV station is probably high, as well. The station's reliability as a news source has suffered a setback, and over the next 48 hours, if Dana keeps her head clear, the whole situation may prove more embarrassing for the paper and the station than for the company.

JOHN R. PURSER *is principal of the Pittsburgh-based consulting firm Purser & Associates, which provides strategic public-affairs counsel to selected corporate clients.*

There are several lessons to be learned from the press situation facing Naturewise, and they are applicable no matter what kind of crisis a company faces. First, top managers must be active participants in the communications function. Second, every company needs a crisis-management plan that kicks in automatically; most crises take an organization by surprise. Third, a crisis-management plan must include established channels of internal communication and a workable strategy for directing and responding to media inquiries.

The media's characterization of Naturewise is clearly unfair; nevertheless, the company faces a crisis that could affect all its internal and external audiences. These days, it is not uncommon for companies to find themselves in such a situation. News reports, whether right or wrong, travel very quickly, and corporate communications departments usually find themselves playing catch-up. The key is to be prepared—to minimize the lag time between the first signs of trouble and a coherent company response. Naturewise is well behind the curve. At Naturewise, everyone's brain seems to have been idling even though television, newspapers, and possibly wire services have been running stories with negative implications about the company for hours. Those responsible for the public relations function have been sitting on their hands, and, as a result, Dana is confronted with a potential retail disaster and investor revolt.

Dana must take charge of the situation, define a strategy, and serve as spokesperson. As a first step, she must quickly put together a response such as the following to stem the flow of negative publicity:

"We deplore the unconscionable bombing of a women's clinic in Joliet, Illinois. Since 1982, Naturewise Apparel has donated more than $4 million to a number of international and domestic relief organizations that support worthy causes, including [list several charities and fax a copy of this statement to those organizations for their use if they are queried]. We rely on nonprofit enterprises like CHICARE to select and distribute donations to organizations that they deem worthy of support. To our knowledge, this is the first instance in which any money that CHICARE distributed has been used for violent purposes.

"As this company's chief executive, I take responsibility for our having failed to investigate thoroughly the backgrounds of charitable organizations to which Naturewise Apparel distributes donations. To ensure that Naturewise is never again associated with an organization that promotes violence, we have instituted a new policy requiring that we research the activities of these enterprises thoroughly before offering support."

Step two is for Dana to begin a series of telephone interviews—first with the reporter from the *Chicago Daily Bulletin*, then with the TV station and the paper that carried the initial stories. In these discussions, she must remain calm, candid, and consistent in her statements.

Concurrently, Bob must provide a written statement to any member of the media looking for a response, and have Dana talk to those who have policy questions he can't answer. He must tell his communications personnel in the field what is happening and give them a copy of the statement, along with an explanatory letter from Dana, for distribution to all employees. It's essential to keep staff members informed as the situation unfolds. Ignoring them in favor of the seemingly more immediate media crisis can have a devastating effect on morale and will result only in rampant rumors and a copy machine working overtime to print résumés. Bob should stress to all employees that they should refer to him any reporters who have questions not answered by the statement.

Meanwhile, Janet needs to arrange conference calls with all Naturewise stores, starting with Chicago-area locations, to explain the company's position and what it is doing to counteract the negative publicity. She should also call CHICARE and urge its representatives to issue a statement condemning the violent act by TermRights and to explain what criteria they use in their charity-selection process. Naturewise may have to exert some pressure on CHICARE to take the lion's share of responsibility in this matter.

After Dana has responded to the most urgent media inquiries, she must contact her potential joint-venture partner and give it a thorough briefing on the situation. It would be helpful if the partner issued a statement affirming that the affair has not diminished its confidence in Naturewise Apparel and its management.

Dana then should reassure all her constituents of the integrity of the company and correct any misconceptions. She must be firm and aggressive with anyone who casts aspersions on her or the company.

Finally, after the crisis has passed, she should fire both Bob and Midwest spokesperson Marc Russo for their incompetence. Bob and Marc should have alerted Dana when the first inquiry was received and offered suggestions on how to handle the problem, not washed their hands of the matter like Pontius Pilate and blindsided her later. In this case, Dana may be able to salvage the situation. But suppose the crisis were of a different nature and Dana couldn't bail them out? Suppose Naturewise faced an unexpected top-management change or a problem with product quality? If the company's communications experts handled this situation so badly, how would they respond in a crisis of potentially greater proportions?

STEPHEN A. GREYSER *is a marketing professor at the Harvard Business School, where he developed and teaches the M.B.A. corporate communications course. He serves on several corporate boards including that of Edel-*

man Worldwide, a public relations firm, and was formerly the chairman of HBR's editorial board.

Dana Osborne is at the center of a potentially volatile situation. Naturewise Apparel is a successful and growing public company that has made its mark on the national scene in part because of its prosocial products and positioning. Thus the positive image of the company would be at risk if its customers believed that Naturewise explicitly supported an organization that publicly undertakes violence. As chief executive, Dana has the opportunity to nip this misconception in the bud and strengthen the company's basic positioning and image.

Her first goal should be damage control—stopping the spread of stories that imply (or permit people to infer) that Naturewise directly supported an organization that instigated violence. It is also vital that she reinforce the company's desired (and existing) image as an involved corporate citizen of the communities in which it operates.

The public of greatest concern to Naturewise is its own customers, many of whom may be attracted to the company by its pro-environment and prosocial stances. (This is the segment that helps sustain The Body Shop; a partially overlapping segment includes Ben & Jerry's patrons.) Consequently, they may be particularly sensitive to negatives such as those in the *Will County Mirror* item (even if that story did find Naturewise Apparel's contribution to the violent group "astonishing"—a word that suggests the newspaper had a generally positive image of the company).

Other pertinent publics are the financial community, which may be helping to finance the overseas expansion, and shareholders. Both are sensitive to negative coverage; witness how Motorola's stock price fell in the wake of alarmist media coverage of allegations that using cellular phones causes cancer. Naturewise employees are another relevant group; for the most part, they just need honest, speedy reassurance.

Before responding to anyone, Dana must focus on the substance of the situation and try to understand how Naturewise got into it. Otherwise, any efforts to communicate could be flawed and lead to greater problems. Consider how Perrier burst its bubble of credibility through a series of changing explanations for why traces of benzene had been found in its bottled water. My speculative analysis is that because this is the first year that Naturewise's regional divisions are handling the donations from the corporate giving fund, they are still moving up the learning curve on "best procedures." The review process for recipient organizations may well be underdeveloped.

So here are my recommendations: Dana should take the call from the Chicago reporter now—even if only to arrange a callback in a short time so that she can prepare for the interview. As a major regional newspaper, the *Chicago Daily Bulletin* offers the potential to reach a large direct audience and—through syndication pickup—an indirect one. It thus provides the opportunity for a positive story about Naturewise direct from its CEO to override the negative story in the *Will County Mirror*. Perhaps Bob Hewitt knows the reporter who called, his beat, or his perspective on business. Such knowledge could help Dana as she thinks about what she wants to say and how she wants to say it.

Then she should question Janet Steiner closely about the decision to fund CHICARE and try to get a handle on what happened when and with whose approval. She should also set in motion a plan for informing her employees of the situation and the company's stance. This can be accomplished by internal means, such as faxed memos to offices and stores and, if necessary, a conference call. The essence of the message should be, "There's a possible problem and here's our position," and Dana should take care to avoid a "sky is falling" attitude. She should also include a contact name and phone number at the home office for any employees who have questions or concerns.

During the interview with the *Chicago Daily Bulletin,* Dana should do three things:

1. Reiterate her endorsement of the company's well-known policy of corporate giving and its rationale. She should cite a total number of millions of dollars donated and say, "We do it because it's the right thing to do." Even if the reporter does not ask her about the corporate-giving policy, Dana must get this information across; it is the cornerstone of the company's position.

2. Admit (it's true!) that Naturewise's Midwest division did give money to CHICARE, "as do many companies in the area." This will illustrate that many others made the same mistake and will take the emphasis off Naturewise. Dana should also say that Naturewise chose CHICARE "because it is involved with so many worthy causes, such as *x.*" She should admit, however, that Naturewise should have been more thorough in checking all of CHICARE's associated groups and say something like, "We didn't know that a group advocating violence was one of its 140 affiliates." She should try to avoid referring to TermRights and its pro-life philosophy, because the focus should be on the violence, which virtually everyone opposes, not on abortion, which is a

divisive issue. Supporting controversial causes and organizations is something most companies avoid because
some of their customers inevitably will be offended.

3. Decry the bombing, "as does every well-meaning
citizen." Dana should emphasize the company's commitment to its core mission and hope for public acceptance
of the regret, particularly in light of Naturewise's image.
My experience is that the public is forgiving if it considers a regret or an apology to be sincere. If she succeeds in
conveying the company's sincerity, the Chicago
reporter's story could well have a "short tail" and be contained in the Midwest. Dana must be prepared, however,
for the possibility of more media coverage. For example,
if someone later dies as a result of the bombing, the story
could resurface with new strength.

At the root of the situation lies the review process for
Naturewise's corporate-giving program. Once Dana has
dealt with the immediate crisis, she will want to conduct a
substantive review of the procedures (probably nonproce-
dures, in my view) that likely led to the Midwest division's
decision to support CHICARE. Some companies think
that "doing good deeds" requires less attention to detail.
This situation can serve as an object lesson.

Moreover, Janet may have thought it safer to support
an umbrella organization. Alas, since umbrella social-
service organizations are largely federations or "distributors," rather than 100% direct service providers, they
have a greater potential than the latter to become
involved in a problem situation.

"Doing good" used to be easier. Today, concerns over
who might be offended by one party's support of another
are much broader than they used to be. Some, for example, opposed giving to the United Way a few years ago
because of the then national CEO's extravagant compen-

sation and benefits package. Family planning is another thorny issue. After AT&T suspended grants to Planned Parenthood to avoid controversy, it discovered that this move, in turn, sparked a negative reaction. Even donations to the Boy Scouts are not immune to protest.

Naturewise's underlying positioning as a caring, environmentally conscious company seems strong, as does its giving policy. Dana should work to fix the process, not the policy or the commitment.

ANNE REYNOLDS WARD *is spokesperson and manager of public affairs for Pepsi-Cola Company in Somers, New York.*

Too many of us in business think of the media as the enemy. They're not. When the media call, you can't hide behind a "no comment" response. The press will report the story with or without you. The sooner you present the facts clearly to the public, the sooner the issue will be resolved. This lesson was reinforced for Pepsi last summer when a single claim of a syringe allegedly discovered in a Diet Pepsi can ignited a nationwide tampering hoax. We knew that by cooperating with, not obstructing, the press, we could get our side of the story out there fast.

In the case of Naturewise, a misleading report has wrongfully linked the company to a violent group and to a potentially deadly terrorist incident. Dana must distance her company from TermRights. She must communicate the integrity of Naturewise and demonstrate that integrity publicly in its defense. She knows that her company had nothing but good intentions in attempting to localize charitable giving, but she also realizes that the public is being told only that dollars are flowing from Naturewise to a violent activist group. The knot is forming in her stomach because she knows that neither she nor her employees have done anything wrong, yet something has gone awry, and the company and its hard-won reputation are in danger.

Because Naturewise did not handle the initial press inquiry astutely, it has already lost valuable time, and the company's reputation has already sustained unnecessary damage. Dana should seize the immediate opportunity to defend her company by presenting the facts in a simple and straightforward way to the Chicago paper. She needs to dispel the notion that her company "funded" the clinic bombing and set the record straight.

The fact is that Naturewise is a victim. The violence at the clinic hurts society *and* the company. Dana must immediately denounce the detestable and irresponsible actions of TermRights and declare that Naturewise does not condone violence for any reason and would never have contributed funds knowingly to any group connected with such tactics. The company has worked hard to build its customers' trust in its innovative products and is recognized for its record of community involvement. It should pledge to review all its contributions and vow to do everything possible to prevent any future funding of groups that advocate violence; for example, it could undertake strict screening measures and encourage employees to be more involved with groups selected to receive funding.

Within the company, Dana should communicate with employees through an open letter that clarifies the facts of the case. The letter should also spell out policy guidelines for contributions and specify the process of evaluating all requests for charitable donations. More important, Dana needs to establish a clear communications policy that defines who speaks to the press on the company's behalf. That policy should include a process for activating a crisis-communications plan in the event things go wrong again.

At Pepsi, a core crisis team of four people is alerted to issues with the potential to escalate. The team—made up of experienced crisis managers from public affairs, regulatory affairs, consumer relations, and operations—assesses each issue, taps into functional experts within Pepsi as needed, and moves quickly to resolve problems and communicate with consumers, regulatory officials, the media, and anyone else affected by the issue. During the syringe scare, the crisis plan worked at warp speed. The first thing Pepsi did was to cooperate with FDA officials and respond openly to the media. Daily advisories to more than 400 Pepsi facilities across the country helped to keep employees informed and business running.

Best case: Dana picks up the phone, gives the Chicago newspaper reporter the facts, and helps the public see her company for what it is—a responsible, innovative organization with great products and strong ties to the communities in which it operates. If she wants to make her position unmistakably clear, she could pledge to restore the damaged property. Although the story will be reported again with more balance, Dana should prepare herself and her company for an imperfect account.

Worst case: Dana panics, decides to let the whole matter drop, and stonewalls press demands. Several things—all bad—might occur in this scenario. First, Naturewise might be linked to the bombing and possibly to any recurrence. The news could spread across the nation and subject the company to greater public scrutiny, a boycott, and potential financial ruin. Internal support could erode as employees begin to feel disenfranchised from the organization they believed in and worked hard for. Groups opposing TermRights' cause and methods could decide to retaliate and put the safety of Naturewise products, employees, and customers in jeopardy. Any hope of support from the public or the press would be lost.

MADGE KAPLAN *is Boston bureau chief for "Marketplace," Public Radio International's program on business and finance. She produces a monthly segment on "Marketplace" called "Think Tank," which is based on articles in HBR.*

There was a time when "no comment" meant simply "no comment." But today when a company spokesperson says "no comment," it implies that the organization has something to hide. Some reporters treat "no comment" as a sort of dare, and the result can be a misleading, unbalanced news story. Without question, Dana should take the call from the *Chicago Daily Bulletin.* Naturewise is not in crisis now, but it will be if she doesn't face the media head-on—and honestly.

If Naturewise had an effective media policy, Dana wouldn't be on the spot right now. But more on that in a moment. Now Dana needs time to gather her thoughts. She should tell the reporter that she is scheduling a press conference for 1 P.M. Pacific time at company headquarters and will answer any questions he has at that time. I suggest 1 P.M. for two reasons. First, it will allow Dana and her staff time to calm down and plan a course of action. Second, most reporters face a late-afternoon deadline, and if Dana wants her views presented accurately, she must give reporters enough time to question her, talk to others, and then go back and file their stories.

When she gets off the phone, Dana should get her administrative assistant to contact the national wire services, regional and national newspapers, and local radio and TV stations about the press conference. The more, the better. The interest from the Chicago paper is a good sign that the story could go national. And because the story—in whatever form it finally takes—will travel thousands of miles fast, Dana must get out in front of it quickly.

Once plans for the press conference are in motion, Dana and her colleagues need to assess the situation. They've been taken by surprise, and right now they're reacting, not thinking. For example, not one of them has said anything about CHICARE's standards. It's hard to believe that such a coalition would have a violent group under its umbrella. Instead of panicking at the thought of press coverage, Dana, Bob, and Janet should be encouraging the media to ask hard questions of the other parties involved and to do their job to get the whole picture. There is more than one story here, and the reporters should be pursuing all the angles.

Of course, Dana should keep in mind that this particular situation may have legal ramifications. There may be charges filed against Naturewise. Dana should consult her corporate lawyer right away, but as a matter of course, not as a defensive knee-jerk measure.

At the press conference, Dana should come right out and say that Naturewise had no idea that CHICARE was funding TermRights. She should admit that something slipped through the cracks and say that Naturewise intends to do everything possible to find out what the slipup was and react appropriately. She should reaffirm

Naturewise's mission and values, and promise that any seeming conflict between those values and funding decisions will be addressed directly.

If a reporter asks her a question she doesn't know the answer to, Dana should say, "I don't know, but I'll find out as soon as possible." She has nothing to gain and everything to lose by dodging or downplaying an issue. A "no comment" forces a reporter to seek other sources for information that Dana should be the one to provide. Dana is Naturewise's best spokesperson; she should not give the press any reason to look elsewhere for "the scoop" on what's happening inside the company.

After this situation has receded, Dana would do well to develop an effective media policy at Naturewise. She might want to think about that policy in almost the same way one thinks about fire drills. In a crisis, people will be reacting, not thinking. And because reporters faced with a deadline don't have the time or the inclination to wait for a company to get its story straight, the organization should have a drill in place to carry it through the initial turmoil generated by an unexpected media spotlight.

For example, why did Marc Russo have nothing to say to the press? Doesn't he have the authority to talk to the media? If not, why have a Midwest communications department? If so, what was his problem? Sure, Marc was surprised by the call. But if a company's core values are clear to everybody in the organization, a regional spokesperson would at least be able to offer a statement like, "We are as shocked as other people to learn that our money went to a group that condones violent actions, and we're looking into it right now. Naturewise would never support violence of any kind." Marc's "no comment" might be an indication that Naturewise needs to work on internal communications.

An effective media policy also means external ground-work, however. As a rule, the more accessible a company's top managers are to the press on a regular basis, the better a company will weather a crisis like the one faced by Naturewise. On television and radio, Dana is the best weapon Naturewise has. The more the public gets to know the company's CEO—her style, her voice, her message—the less likely it will be to pass judgment quickly and severely when an errant report surfaces.

As for the local news story, I'm appalled that any editor would have let a piece like that run. It's unfortunate that so many so-called news organizations will publish a sensational story rather than take the time to conduct balanced, thoughtful reporting. Why didn't the reporter from the *Will County Mirror* question CHICARE as well as Naturewise? Why did he or she never try to contact Naturewise headquarters? That kind of shoddy reporting turns my stomach, but it's out there.

Top managers should also keep in mind, however, that if they are not happy with the coverage they are getting, they can always let the media know what they think. Call the editor. Open a channel. Investing the time to clear up confusion and get acquainted will set the stage for future good relations and fair reporting. Shutting up tight won't.

Kids' Store Funded Clinic Bombers

A $120 MILLION retail-clothing chain funded the group that has claimed responsibility fo Monday's bombing of a Joliet abortion clinic, the *Will County Mirror* has learned.

Naturewise Apparel, which is based in Seattle and has regional headquarters in Chicago, provided support money to TermRights, the pro-life group claiming responsibility for the bombing. In January, the company contributed $150,000 to CHICARE, an umbrella social service organization. TermRights is one of the groups supported by CHICARE.

With 212 stores nationwide, Naturewise currently commands 1% of the children's casual-clothing market in the United States. Last year, it enjoyed sales increase of 12%. The company has built a reputation as a "green" organization. CEO Dana Osborne founded the chain after her daughter developed a serious skin condition caused by the synthetic fibers in her clothing. Naturewise's apparel has always been chemical-free and made only of natural fibers. Perhaps because of its roots, the company has consistently supported environmental causes and antiviolence/anticrime drives on the national level.

Naturewise's contribution to TermRights is astonishing given the company's usual politically correct stance. TermRights publicly condones violence in support of its cause. In fact, the group has claimed responsibility for several violent acts against abortion clinics over the past two years.

Naturewise refused to respond to questions from the *Will County Mirror.*

Originally published in July–August 1994
Reprint 94407

After the Layoffs, What Next?

SUZY WETLAUFER

Executive Summary

HARRY DENTON, THE CEO in this fictional case study, has been caught off guard. As the head of Delarks, a venerable department-store chain in the Midwest, he has engineered a remarkable turnaround in only a year. Sales have rebounded, and Wall Street is applauding. Sure, a few trees were felled in the process—to make room for new growth, Denton had to clear out 3,000 pieces of what he privately refers to as "deadwood"—but he'd saved the company. Didn't people understand that?

Not exactly. When Delarks's head of merchandising defects to a competitor, Denton is shocked to realize that many of the survivors, in fact, have had it with him and with the company. The last straw was the recent closing of the Madison store, which Denton announced without warning to anyone—not even the company's head of HR, Thomas Wazinsky, a supposedly trusted adviser. In the wake of that coup, store employees from Wichita to Peoria are wondering, Are we next? The rumor mill says that many of them are considering leaving before Denton can inflict the next blow. And senior managers are not immune to the fear and anger. Even Wazinsky, one of the few links to Delarks's proud past, confesses to Denton, "I'll bet you're thinking of firing me."

Denton has to act—and fast. He calls a "town meeting" for the 600 employees of the St. Paul store. The plan: rally the troops. Instead, Denton is routed. Angry questions are hurled at the CEO, and he is forced to beat a hasty retreat through the back door.

Five experts offer advice on how to revive morale at the successful but troubled company.

"PERIWINKLE, DEFINITELY periwinkle." Claire Ladd's insistent voice filled the room, but it was greeted with dead silence.

"Did you hear me, Harry? I said *periwinkle*. It's *the* color of the fall season. And Harry, no suits this year. We're seeing all separates out of Milan, Paris, and Seventh Avenue. The woman's suit is dead."

Harry Denton shook his head and stared blankly at the woman across his desk. He knew he should be paying attention to her. After all, Claire Ladd represented a major apparel distributor for Delarks, the Chicago-based department-store chain of which he was CEO. But ever since Denton had read that morning's *Women's Wear Daily*, he had been unable to concentrate on anything but the headline stripped across the top of the second page: "Delarks Merchandising Chief Defects—Will Others Follow?"

Ladd walked around Denton's desk and gently shook him by the shoulders. In the 20-odd years they had known each other, starting when they were both "rack runners" in New York's bustling garment district, their relationship had always been honest—and even familial. "Snap out of it, Harry!" she laughed. "I'm not hawking periwinkle sweater sets for my health. Are we going to place orders here today or not?" When there was no immediate response, Ladd leaned closer, looking at Denton quizzically. "I mean, Harry," she said, "I was expecting a big order from you—everyone says Delarks is soaring again. You saved the chain. You're a hero on Wall Street. And when I was walking through the Springfield store last week, the place was filled with customers. It was packed—not like the old days, when you could set off a cannon in there and no one would notice. And Harry, the customers: they were *buying*. We like that."

Denton sighed. He liked it too. In fact, he loved it, as did the company's board of directors. Just that Monday, they had informed him that his contract had been renewed for two more years, with an increased salary and more stock options. They were delighted with his performance—and with Delarks. In just one year, Denton had transformed Delarks from a boring, outdated chain that catered to "aging dowager princesses," as Denton called them, into a fun, chic shopping emporium for the Midwest's growing population of affluent female baby boomers. The 28-store chain, with shops in small and midsize cities such as Bismarck, North Dakota, and Peoria, Illinois, had been

The problem, Denton knew, was that Delarks's transformation had involved quite a bit of bloodshed.

on the verge of bankruptcy when Harry was lured away from his job running a national chain's flagship store in Manhattan. Now Delarks's success was the talk of the retail industry, in large part due to a leap in revenues to $400 million and the accompanying 20% surge in the chain's stock price. But the truth was, success wasn't tasting as sweet as Denton had hoped it would.

The problem, Denton knew, was that Delarks's transformation had involved quite a bit of bloodshed in the form of layoffs. Turnarounds always do; Denton had made that clear to his direct reports in his first week on the job. His strategy included refurbishing dowdy-looking stores and slashing overhead to meet the huge remodeling costs. And the strategy emphasized

The survivors were angry. Many thought Denton should have held meetings before the layoffs to warn people they were coming.

the need for a highly trained sales force that could execute "link selling," in which shoppers who enter the store looking for one product end up leaving with five, and feeling happy about it to boot. Link selling meant that "deadwood"—a term he never used publicly, of course— would have to be cleared out to make room for a new breed of sophisticated, energized sales associates.

In other words, Denton told himself, layoffs had been inevitable. Especially at a company like Delarks, which had for years been run by an old-fashioned, even patriarchal, group of managers led by the founder's son. Even after Delarks went public in 1988 and hired some new senior managers, the chain boasted salaries and benefits that were out of line for the industry, as well as a no-layoff policy.

Denton was well aware of that policy when he made the decision to cut Delarks's employment rolls by 20%, about 3,000 people in all. Some of the layoffs were less painful than others. For instance, most people understood that the chain's in-store restaurants had to be shut down. Gone were the days when women had time for a leisurely lunch as they shopped. The restaurants were rarely busy; closing them eliminated about 400 jobs. The consolidation of several half-empty distribution centers was also widely accepted by the organization. But people seemed to take the firing of several hundred longtime saleswomen very hard. Denton had predicted such a reaction, but he knew he had no choice: many of the old-timers were the lowest producers. And they had neither the abilities required for link selling nor a feel for the new kind of merchandise Delarks was offering: urban, modern, and trendy.

The pink slips had gone out on a Friday morning before lunch. That was the way Denton had always done it; indeed, it was the way he had always seen it done in the industry. It gave people time to clean out their desks and say their goodbyes before the end of the day. It also gave the survivors a weekend to cool off before returning to work. Denton wasn't coldhearted about the process, but having lived through about a dozen downsizings in his career, he believed there was really no "kinder, gentler" way to fire people. The best approach was to do it quickly and in one fell swoop, and to make sure that everyone received a fair severance package. In fact, Denton believed he had gone beyond fair. The laid-off employees had been given two months pay and free outplacement services for one month, practically an unheard-of deal in the retail industry.

Denton's view was that when a company is in financial trouble and a new CEO is brought in, everyone knows that layoffs are next.

Still, the reaction had been severe. Not so much from the fired people; most of them went quietly. But the survivors were angry, and even the new staff Denton had brought in with him were upset. Many thought he should have held meetings before the layoffs to warn people they were coming. But he had rejected that idea. His view was that when a company is in deep financial trouble and a new CEO is brought in to save it, everyone knows that layoffs are next. Why make matters worse by rubbing their noses in it?

But now Denton was nervous. The wounds opened by the layoffs were not healing. In the newspaper article about Rachel Meyer's defection, the reporter had speculated that the move by Delarks's head of merchandising was connected to the downsizing initiative. The company was a morass of bad feelings, the article suggested, although Meyer had said "no comment" when asked directly about morale at the company.

An anonymous source quoted in the article had been more forthcoming. "There's no trust at Delarks," the source had said. "People feel like senior management isn't honest with its people. They just want to fix up the company fast and mop up the damage later." Denton felt stung. Who had said that? Was it someone from inside? Denton felt he *had* been honest, although maybe in the rush of executing the turnaround he hadn't done enough to prove it.

"This company is a mess, Claire," Denton blurted out. "I feel like everything I've built in the last year is collapsing around me."

"What—you've got to be kidding!"

Denton pulled the newspaper out of his desk drawer and showed it to her. "Rachel Meyer is leaving," he said, "and she's walking right across the street to Blake and

Company. That's bad on its own, but what if she takes other people with her? What if she takes Liz Garcia?"

Ladd frowned. Garcia was Delarks's director of sales-associate training and one of the main reasons for the chain's turnaround. Denton had brought her with him from New York, and she had performed just as expected, giving Delarks's sales associates the savvy, direction, and skills they needed to connect with the company's new clientele. Her contribution was critical, especially because Denton had switched the salespeople's compensation system from one based on salary to one based on commission.

"You can't lose Liz," Ladd said quietly. "Harry, I'm going to get out of here so you can take care of the business that really matters now. Can we meet in a week?"

Denton nodded. "Thanks, Claire," he said. "Maybe I'll have stopped the bleeding by then."

But by the next day, the bleeding was worse. Garcia was still on board. But Thomas Wazinsky, Delarks's head of HR, told Denton that rumors were flying: four or five other senior people were supposedly on their way out, including the head of the profitable store in Wichita, Kansas. And there was also talk that "legions" of salespeople were packing up to leave the company.

"Is this just talk?" Denton pressed Wazinsky. "Have you received any official resignations?"

"No—no letters," Wazinsky allowed. "But Harry, you've got to realize, people are terribly unhappy. Morale is really low."

"That's not what you told me when we paid $20,000 for that employee attitude survey!" Denton snapped. "It didn't say people were ready to quit in droves." Three months earlier, Wazinsky had hired a small, local consulting firm to take the pulse of the company's employees.

The results showed that pockets of employees were disaffected but that most were satisfied with the chain's new strategy. The consulting firm said that the results were typical for a company going through a downsizing, and even a bit more positive than usual. But it also recommended that Denton get out into the organization soon, both to reassure people that there would be no more layoffs and to explain the ones that had been necessary.

Denton had taken part of the advice. He did visit about half of the stores, and he did explain why Delarks had laid people off, but he refused to promise that there would be no more layoffs. In a turnaround situation, Denton knew, you have to leave your options open. And in fact, Denton had been right not to make assurances. Four weeks after his visits to the field, he decided to shut the chain's worst-performing store, in Madison, Wisconsin, eliminating another 200 jobs. After that, Denton felt relatively sure that the downsizing of Delarks was over, but again, he thought it would be unwise to make that news public. Too risky.

Now Denton was reconsidering: the time may have come to tell people that no more layoffs were impending. He tried the idea out on Wazinsky.

"I doubt people will believe you," he replied. Wazinsky was one of the few executives left over from the old regime. A native of Minnesota, he had been with the chain nearly 30 years, his entire career. Denton felt as though Wazinsky had never warmed to him and at times had even wondered if he should let him go. But he had decided a few months ago that Wazinsky, on balance, was a very valuable resource: he was keyed in to the organization in a way that Denton was not. It sometimes seemed, in fact, as if Wazinsky knew every single employee in the company on a first-name basis.

"Harry, can I be straight with you?" Wazinsky asked.

"Of course. Aren't you always?"

Wazinsky shrugged. "I might as well go for broke here, since I think my days are numbered—"

"Are you quitting?" Harry cut him off.

"No," Wazinsky said, "but I bet you're thinking of firing me."

An awkward silence filled the CEO's office.

"You're not going to be fired, I promise you that," Denton said finally. He meant it, and as he said the words, he was struck by how much trouble he was in if even Wazinsky didn't trust him. After all, the two of them spoke every day, often about the most confidential details of the turnaround strategy. The one exception had been the closing of the Madison store. Denton hadn't told anyone about that in advance except for members of the board, for fear of the news leaking to the press before the employees heard officially.

"I guess I should have told you beforehand about Madison," Denton acknowledged.

"Madison was a big screwup, if you don't mind my saying," Wazinsky replied with a rueful smile. "Yes, you should have told me—and you should have told Sylvia O'Donnell, the store manager. She should *not* have gotten her letter along with everyone else. People aren't going to forget that." Wazinsky paused, then went on. "I mean, Harry, there are stories going all around this company about the day Madison closed. They say people ran into Sylvia's office after the announcement and found her sitting there in shock, shaking her head and saying, 'I had no idea,' over and over again."

"I was just trying to make sure people didn't find out through the press or the grapevine," Denton quietly protested.

"Well, whatever you were trying to do doesn't matter now," said Wazinsky. "It backfired."

"So now what?" Denton asked with a short laugh. "I mean, it's crazy, isn't it? Sales are up, and I just got our last quarter's results a few days ago. We're going to have solid profits by year's end. But if the rumors are true, our great big success is going to shrink in a hurry."

The two men stared at each other, lost in thought. Then both started to talk at once. They were struck by the same plan: to hold a series of "town meetings" at every store in the chain, in which Denton would talk straight with the employees. He would promise no more layoffs, apologize for the ways those in the past had been handled, and set the tone for the company's future. "We need to clear the air," Denton said. "People should be celebrating around here, not complaining."

The first town meeting was called for two days later in one of the chain's largest stores, in St. Paul, Minnesota. All 600 employees were invited to attend the session, which was held in the conference room of a hotel in downtown St. Paul, near the store.

"I'll be honest with you. I probably should have handled the downsizing differently—" Denton was cut off by raucous applause.

As he surveyed the crowd before going on stage, it looked to Denton as if all 600 employees were there. He couldn't help but notice that the room was remarkably quiet. There was tension in the air.

Denton was tense, too. At the airport in Chicago earlier that day, Wazinsky had approached him with a pained look. "Harry, I just listened to a voice mail from Liz," he said. "She wants to meet with you as soon as possible."

"How bad is it?" Denton demanded. "Is she leaving?"

"Well, she says she can't stand working in a place where everyone hates coming to work. My guess is she's considering joining Rachel across the street."

Now, several hours later, Denton tried to block out his concerns about Liz and summon up his confidence. He cleared his throat and began speaking. "Delarks is a retail chain to be proud of again," he said, "thanks to you. In the past 18 months, there have been many changes in the way Delarks does business. What we asked of you wasn't easy—far from it—but you rose to the challenge and made success happen."

Denton had expected applause at that line, but there wasn't any. He moved on to the hard part: the layoffs. "I'll be honest with you," he began, "I probably should have handled the downsizing differently—"

Here, he *was* cut off by applause, raucous and prolonged. He waited until it died down, and continued. "Layoffs are never easy. I'm not even sure there is a 'right' way to do them. But I take full responsibility for doing them in a way that felt wrong to a lot of you."

Again, the room broke into loud applause. But Denton could tell the applause wasn't a positive release of energy: people looked angry. He decided to cut his losses and move right into the question and answer period.

He didn't recognize the first person to approach the microphone—a middle-aged man in a plaid flannel shirt. Denton figured he was someone from the stockroom.

"Delarks may be making a lot of money now, Mr. Denton," he said pointedly, "but it's not a family anymore. It doesn't feel right. You and your folks from New York are always hiding up there on the eighteenth floor. You don't care anything about the people who are earning your big salaries for you."

Again, cheers.

The man continued, "You just fired people like Mae Collier without any warning. Just up and fired her. That woman gave her whole life to Delarks. She was like a mother to a lot of us, especially the girls on the sales floor. You treated her like a hired hand. That's not right. You broke the heart of the store that day."

Denton had no idea who Mae Collier was, and the truth probably showed on his face. She had been a saleswoman, obviously, and most likely one who had low sales per square foot. But beyond that . . .

"Is Mae coming back?" the man at the microphone interrupted Denton's thoughts.

Denton hadn't expected this. He knew he would have to handle tough questions about how he had managed the downsizing. He had even expected that he would have to grovel about how he had botched the Madison closing. But to be questioned about an individual employee like this Mae Collier—that was not something he had prepared for.

"You just fired people like Mae Collier without any warning. You broke the heart of the store that day."

He stalled for a moment, but he knew there was no point trying to placate the crowd with some sort of fudged half-truth. When he spoke, his answer was simple. "No," he said, "Mae Collier is not coming back. None of the employees who were let go are coming back. Delarks is a different store now, and we need to let go of the past and focus on the future, and our future is very bright."

Another member of the audience pushed her way to the microphone. "People are *hurting*, Mr. Denton," she almost shouted. "You can't talk about the future with us until you make up for the past."

"That's what I'm trying to do right now," he shot back, exasperated. "What do you think I'm standing up here for?"

No one answered directly, but the crowd was rumbling unhappily. Denton was about to speak again when Wazinsky appeared at his shoulder and pulled him back from the podium. "Don't dig yourself in any deeper," he whispered. "Wrap it up. Say you're sorry and let's get out of here."

Denton turned back to the crowd, ready to close the meeting with an appeal: give me chance, he wanted to say. But, looking out, he could see people were already filing toward the door. No one would listen to him anyway. He shut off his microphone and followed Wazinsky to a back exit of the hotel.

What should Delarks do to repair the damage caused by a mismanaged downsizing?

Five experts offer advice on how to revive morale at the successful but troubled company.

BOB PEIXOTTO *is vice president for total quality and human resources at L.L. Bean in Freeport, Maine.*

Harry Denton is increasingly isolated from the company he has chosen to lead. He has put strategy *before* people, when his people should have been an integral part of the strategy. In his quest for a bold turnaround, he has broken trust at every turn. Thomas Wazinsky speaks for the entire company when he confides, "I think my days are numbered. I bet you're thinking of firing me." Faced with fear and distrust and the imminent defections of top-level people, Denton needs to do the following:

Stabilize key people. He must carefully assess his senior staff, deciding how much he trusts each person and determining the value that each brings to the company. Then he should sit down with them privately and acknowledge his mistakes and what he has learned. He should express his confidence in them, his desire to have each person on his team, and his vision for Delarks's future—including what's in it for them. Finally, he should ask for each person's commitment. Straight talk, heartfelt expressions of confidence, and a picture of an engaging future are more powerful motivators than any retention bonus.

Appoint a "change cosponsor." Delarks has undergone a drastic restructuring. A CEO can rarely lead a change of such magnitude alone. Denton needs help. He should ask Wazinsky to cosponsor the company's change efforts.

As one of the few executives remaining from the old regime, Wazinsky seems to have unique credibility with the company's employees. If he is seen embracing the changes at Delarks, the whole effort will be viewed in a new light by the frontline people. But Denton will first have to heal the breach in trust that he opened up when he failed to tell Wazinsky about his plan to close the Madison store.

Clarify the change message. Although the downsizing is over with, Denton and his senior team need to develop a brief, compelling message that includes three elements: the case for change, a view of the future, and a commitment to what will not change. Everyone in the management team should know the message well and repeat it often.

The people at Delarks need to understand the case for change: how the industry changed and why the company needed to respond. Denton may want to go beyond the message, in fact, to launch an education program that would enrich people's understanding of the business, demonstrate commitment to their development, and show trust by sharing information. By creating business-savvy employees, the program would also make future efforts to change easier.

The view of the future should describe the key elements of the change: the refurbishment of stores, the repositioning of the product line, link selling, and the new compensation system for sales associates. It should make clear the desired outcome of the changes, and it must be based on values that the people at Delarks can embrace.

Finally, Denton needs to spend some time alone thinking about what will not change. He's already rejected Delarks's former customers as "aging dowager princesses" and its longtime employees as "deadwood." One can bet that these "private" confidences have spread widely enough to become legendary. Denton needs to find something about Delarks's past that he can personally appreciate and publicly revere, something he can use as a cornerstone for the company's future. Delarks's people need to know that Denton values their past efforts.

Communicate, communicate, communicate. Communication must be constant, candid, and two-way. Denton has been assuming that people understand his intentions. But, because of the company's longstanding policy against layoffs, they were not anticipating the downsizing. And many may not have recognized the company's deep financial troubles or the way the marketplace was changing. A 20% surge in the stock price has not been nearly as important to people deep in the organization as the trust, long-term relationships, and predictability that used to exist. Denton needs to develop listening posts to stay in touch with his organization. At L.L. Bean, for example, we sample reactions to potential changes from a specially selected panel of employees.

Denton should also resume the town meetings. In 1995, following a voluntary reduction in the workforce at Bean, company president Leon Gorman conducted 27 town meetings over a two-week period. Nearly a third of each meeting was reserved for questions from the audience. This was the richest part of each meeting. It let frontline people vent their feelings and know that they had been heard.

Invest in the survivors. Delarks must create a way to help the sales force change. New performance expectations need to be clear and linked to the business case. The company has a golden opportunity to signal real trust in its frontline people by asking them to help define the competencies required for link selling. Top employees can be tapped as trainer-coaches to help their peers. Denton is likely to be surprised by the emergence of a group of energized leaders of change.

Drive out fear and build in trust. Denton should remove as much uncertainty as possible by declaring layoffs a last resort and by being clear about how decisions affecting individuals and stores will be made. People should understand that layoffs are not random acts and that their strong performance and support for the company's new directions can limit their vulnerability.

At the same time, it doesn't make strategic sense for Denton to assure people that there will never again be layoffs. No one would believe him. The only promises the company's leaders should be making are short-term tangible ones that can be kept.

Keep the spirit of change alive. Communication should
not be limited to a onetime town-meeting blitz. Delarks's
leaders need to repeat frequently the key points about
the change effort. Frontline people need continual
opportunities to vent their feelings. New information
about the company's direction should be delivered to
employees regularly. Such updates can occur at team
meetings and should focus on measurable goals and
clear milestones; and questions should be welcome. As
progress, small wins, and new behaviors are celebrated, a
renewed sense of energy and momentum will carry
Delarks to higher levels of prosperity.

> JIM EMSHOFF *is CEO of IndeCap Enterprises, a consult-
> ing firm based in Lake Forest, Illinois.*

I'm surprised that Denton has been so successful in
improving Delarks's performance. Generally, a company
whose staff is unraveling wouldn't experience this kind
of turnaround.

That does not mean I think Denton is some sort of
miracle manager. To restore his employees' trust and
rebuild morale, he has serious work to do. But let me be
very clear about what he should *not* do: under no circumstances should Denton backpedal or pretend to "start
over" with his current staff. He should definitely not hold
another town meeting or any other event in which
Delarks's employees are encouraged to rehash the blood-
letting they have just lived through.

Why not? Because whether or not any of the employees realize it, they have all been through the toughest
part of the restructuring. Denton has already convinced
the employees, old and new, that if Delarks hadn't
changed, it would be bankrupt. That's why he has a shiny

new sales force in place. That's why he has successfully changed the merchandise and the way the stores are operated. And that's why, in an amazingly short time, Wall Street is taking notice. Saying to employees, "Trust me—when we get through this, we're going to have a stronger company," is difficult. Many senior managers fail to get this point across in turnarounds. Denton, somehow, has succeeded.

No, this is not the time to look back. Instead, Denton must begin to capitalize, in a very tangible way, on the solid foundation he has built. Specifically, he should focus on three things.

First, capitalize on the company's financial strength. The company's stock price—and its sales—are up. The stock may be rising on the early part of an S curve; it may shoot up even more rapidly in the near future. Denton needs to share that success with his senior management team by giving them a large stock-option award, phased in over five years. He needs to make sure that they have an incentive to remain with the company through thick and thin.

He should also open up an option or stock-grant program for all Delarks employees. People need to understand that the changes at Delarks are not just skin deep—that the company is no longer the old-school, paternalistic place it once was. And the way to do that is to let them into the organization's heart. Denton should want his employees to understand exactly what the restructuring was all about; he should want them to be looking at the financial pages in their newspapers and doing the math.

You can't work as a loner when you hold the top job in any organization.

The sales staff, the stock clerks, and the sanitary workers should see how a stock uptick means they will have that much more money for their retirement or for their children's college tuitions.

The sales associates need particular attention. If the commission program was designed properly, they should be taking in much more money than they did under Delarks's salary system. But Denton must make sure that the salespeople are drawing the right conclusions. They should understand that the commission program is a real, positive change resulting from the restructuring.

Second, rebuild a cohesive senior management team. Build, in fact, might be a better term; it's not clear that Denton ever had a proper leadership team to begin with.

Denton is a loner, that much is certain. His way of keeping people in the dark has been largely responsible for all the free-floating anxiety in the organization. The fact is, you can't work as a loner when you hold the top job in any organization. This seems to be Denton's first leadership position, and anyone in a new job needs time to learn and adjust. Even so, Denton must change the way he manages.

He should start by focusing on Liz Garcia. After all, she came with him to this company. She had faith in him at some point—enough to leave another job—and she has been successful at Delarks. Denton should bring her in and say, "Look, we've crossed phase one of this thing, now the fun can begin. I want you to take the lead in building the next-generation plan for the sales associates. I'm making you responsible for tweaking the commission program to encourage cooperation among the salespeople. I'm here to help, and so is Wazinsky." And

Denton should ask her some challenging questions. Can we rehire some of the old sales associates and retrain them in the new system? Do you think virtually all the stores' customers are new? Should the company segment its sales force? Have we missed other opportunities to turn the staff into a team? These assignments should remotivate Garcia. What she needs is an opportunity to move from being a trainer to becoming an integral part of the company's senior-leadership team. I would be surprised if, after receiving Denton's proposal, she didn't decide to stay at Delarks.

When Garcia is back on board, Denton should turn to the rest of the senior managers. Holding an off-site session dedicated to sharing the senior group's knowledge about Delarks and defining the innovations needed to take the company to the next level would set things right quickly. I would strongly recommend that Denton hire a facilitator to help him run the session. He doesn't need a repeat of the town meeting. But the senior management team probably will be no larger than 15 people, and he can use the meeting to bring them together. The way he announces the stock option plan, for example, can help bond the group.

The key will be letting his managers know that he understands how Delarks fits in with their careers and with their lives in general, and that their experience should be both challenging and enjoyable. And he should impress upon them that he wants them to become the agents of a new culture that travels down through the organization.

Third, create a permanent communication process for all Delarks employees. When I was CEO of Diner's Club, we had a successful program, and my suggestions stem from that. Denton should start a program called

Take Stock in Delarks. If he follows my first recommendation, all Delarks employees will be stockholders and thus will be doubly interested in the company. To capitalize on that interest, he should issue a quarterly report on progress and challenges and then use the reports as a vehicle to generate discussions in individual stores. Subsequently, he can report on what he has learned and any employee ideas he has implemented, thus strengthening the connection between management and staff. Denton might also consider hosting an annual meeting or celebration as part of the program.

It will probably be a couple of years before the program takes hold—that is, before employees believe that the program isn't a gimmick. But if Denton takes my first two suggestions to heart, resolves to keep his focus on the future, and stops playing the lone ranger, morale should improve to the point that it mirrors those amazing turnaround numbers.

RICHARD MANNING *is the former editor of the* Boston Business Journal *and* New England Business *magazine. He is now a writer, editor, and consultant north of Boston.*

Denton needs to start all over again where he should have started in the first place: with his employees. And he needs to start with a display of honesty and forthrightness that so far has been incredibly lacking on his part.

The first thing he has to do is stop the bleeding. He has to send out a companywide memo that says two things: the layoffs are over, period, and I'll soon be visiting all 28 stores to meet with all the company's employees. If a copy of the memo ends up on page one of the next day's *Chicago Tribune*, well, that's simply a risk that Denton will have to take. His main problem has been isolation, after all, and anything that will bring him closer to his workforce will redound to the company's benefit. Even a press leak.

Denton needs to explain to his people in the memo that from the outset he had the equation upside down. The memo might look something like this:

"I felt that the way to turn the company around lay along the course of improving infrastructure, improving the product, and improving merchandising. And I was wrong in that assumption, because the assumption ignored the development of the company's most important assets: its employees.

"I realized this suddenly over the last few days when I learned that the head of merchandising was leaving, the head of HR was totally demoralized, and the chief of sales-associate training was poised to jump. I'd become so enmeshed in the balance sheet that I thought I could take the pulse of the company's most important assets by commissioning something as preposterous as an employee attitude survey. Such surveys are nothing but an invitation to dissemble, shrug, and flatter, and they often have no bearing on reality.

Denton has to send out a memo that says the layoffs are over, period.

"What I have ignored all along is that in any corporation, large or small, the most important assets all wear shoes. They walk if you tell them to—as I've told 3,000 to do in the past year—or they walk if they're scared for their jobs. No steel mill, no law firm, no clothing retailer will be able to prosper if the assets that wear shoes are not managed the same way a prudent manager manages merchandising, infrastructure, and other parts of the business.

"This has been my greatest failing so far. In admitting that, I am putting my rear where I know everyone else's been all along: on the line. I should have been in Peoria and Bismarck and Madison talking with employees at the very outset, but I was not. I've been relying on outside consultants and managing in the splendid isolation of the eighteenth floor. And I've just come to the terrible realization that no matter what I do with the ledgers, if the company's assets decide to vote with their feet, there will be no company left. Dresses don't sell dresses. People sell dresses. People unload trucks. People stock stockrooms. People work cash registers.

The memo might say this: "If the company's assets decide to vote with their feet, there will be no company left."

"I've been blissfully ignorant of those truths for the past year, and it's my fault that morale is low and that people are talking about leaving in droves. To get things back to where they should be, Thomas Wazinsky, our head of HR, will organize employee feedback circles at each of the stores. The purpose of the circles will be to come up with ideas about how to make the company work better and to let employees know they have a real say in how the company operates. Store managers will present the circles' findings at monthly meetings at headquarters in Chicago.

"'Meaningful work,' to quote William Butler Yeats, 'is not the filling of a pail but the lighting of a fire.' I want Delarks people to know they can light fires at the company."

GUN DENHART *is the founder and chair of Hanna Andersson Corporation, a children's clothing direct-mail company in Portland, Oregon.*

I don't believe that all is lost for Denton. At least not yet. But if he is to save Delarks, he must act fast, and his first priority must be rebuilding his employees' trust—in him and in the company.

First, I would suggest that he try again to meet with small groups of employees throughout the organization. He must be honest with them. No manager can promise a completely rosy future, and so he can't guarantee that there will never be another layoff at Delarks. But he should tell them that if the need ever arises again—if Delarks finds itself in a position in which downsizing is the only way to ensure survival—the situation will be handled much, much differently. And he should promise that employees will be kept up-to-date on the company's performance so that they will never again be blindsided.

It might be a good idea if Denton began these meetings with an apology. And at some point in the meeting, perhaps after he has assured people that there will be no more layoffs in the current restructuring, he should give them a chance to talk. People need to show their emotions, and Denton should let them do so without getting defensive. He should just listen until everyone who wants to speak has had a say.

I realize that that will be very difficult for him. He does not strike me as the kind of person who is sensitive in that way—who knows when to talk and when to listen. But perhaps he can prepare a bit beforehand—by role-playing with someone, for example—or at least make sure that his HR director is by his side at the meetings to raise a warning finger if he begins to get defensive or to talk over his employees.

Denton must understand, before hosting these meetings, that people are going to be very angry and that given the opportunity, in a safe forum, they will vent their true feelings. But he must also understand that anger is not going to be the only emotion fueling the storm. The employees who remain at Delarks are probably feeling quite a bit of guilt as well. After all, some of their closest friends—people with lifelong careers at the company—are now looking for work, while they still collect their pay. He must be ready to acknowledge that guilt and to take on some of it as his own.

When a meeting is over, Denton should hand out a letter to each employee that confirms his apology and his assurance that such a mismanaged downsizing will never again occur. That Denton means what he says and is ready to stand by his word must be made very real to everyone who attends.

The meetings are just a start. To follow through on his promises, Denton must change his management style. Specifically, that means visiting his stores on a regular basis. Getting to know employees' names and histories. Keeping people informed about the state of the business. Delarks employees should know if the stores are doing well or poorly. They should know why, and they should have a way to tell Denton what works at Delarks and what does not. In other words, they must be active participants in Denton's strategy for success, not just tools.

Denton's new management style must also include a commitment to communication—in both directions—with his senior management team. It is unconscionable that he did not inform his HR director or the manager in Madison that he was going to shut down that store. Denton has a great problem with trust. He has to realize that none of his employees will ever trust him unless he begins to trust them.

At least Denton realizes that something is dreadfully wrong at Delarks, and he wants to make things right. To that end, I would recommend that he contact Business for Social Responsibility, an organization based in San

Francisco whose mission is to help managers achieve commercial success while maintaining the highest possible respect for people, the community, and the environment. With that help, and with some hard work, he may be able to salvage what was once a strong, positive company culture.

SAUL GELLERMAN *is a management psychologist in Irving, Texas, and the former dean of the Graduate School of Management at the University of Dallas.*

I'd fault Delarks's board of directors more than Denton for what looks like an impending disaster. Denton is a former store manager with no prior experience as a CEO. Without an informed mentor—someone who can ask tough questions and demand thoughtful answers—an inexperienced CEO can turn into a loose cannon, as Denton did.

There's no evidence of oversight by the board on Denton's decisions. It was content to look at the numbers, never inquiring whether they were sustainable or what the costs and risks of achieving them were. In brief, the board's governance was superficial and helped create this looming fiasco.

That said, the immediate question is, What's best for Delarks now?

In the short run, nothing is going to change the fact that Delarks lacks an effective leader. Denton lost much of his credibility when he axed the entire Madison store without warning. That shock made the isolated gripes of the disaffected few suddenly seem all too valid to the previously silent majority. It left the survivors anxious and cynical. After the Madison massacre, they probably lived in dread of Fridays. And after the St. Paul meeting, where Denton did more preaching than listening, they most likely lost all faith in the CEO.

The company still needs Denton's strategic guidance, but it needs someone else to implement his strategy on a day-to-day basis. In brief, Delarks needs someone to front for Denton, someone the frontline troops will believe.

The only senior executive in the case who could play that role convincingly is the head of HR, Wazinsky. His job title should be changed to executive vice president. But Denton should make this appointment with his eyes open, because Wazinsky—although he may have the respect of Delarks's employees—was not a strong HR director.

First, he settled for an amateurish employee-attitude survey. His consultants focused on a side issue—how morale at Delarks compared with that of other downsizing firms—and never got down to the key question: What issues were driving the "disaffection" that burst out of its "pockets" like a virus when Denton made his big blunder and closed the Madison store?

Second, there is no evidence that Wazinsky warned Denton that Delarks would be wide open to an age discrimination suit if he based mass layoffs on anything but performance. Firing "several hundred longtime saleswomen" like Mae Collier could come back to haunt Denton in ways that he fails to recognize.

Nevertheless, the appointment of Wazinsky would at least temporarily calm a very troubled organization. The message Wazinsky should try to convey is that while the good old days are gone forever, the company will cling to its original core values—decency and respect for each employee—even as it sheds some outdated values—the guaranteed job security and disregard for change that characterized the old Delarks.

Keeping Denton behind the scenes is a first step, but not the last. To rescue Denton's career at Delarks, the board's chair would have to intervene. Specifically, he or she would have to insist that Denton agree to cooperate with a consultant of the chair's choosing. In other words, Denton would have to want to fight on at Delarks so much that he would be willing to work with an outsider to learn a new management style.

If Denton does not agree to this course of action, the board would be better off owning up to its mistake. It should buy out his contract and shop around for a more thoughtful CEO. Of course, that implies major disruptions on the board itself. But that's the price of looking only at results and ignoring how they were achieved.

Fortunately, Denton already seems open to change. He's upset and knows that he's in trouble, both of which are good signs. They mean he's beginning to face the possibility that his own decisions are at the root of his difficulties.

One final point. Whenever you contemplate firing people, whether you're letting a single individual go or carrying out a massive downsizing, the most important consideration is always this: How will your decision affect the survivors? If morale plummets, you could lose your best people and get only the minimum effort from those left behind. In short, no economic gains for a lot of psychological pain.

Originally published in September–October 1998
Reprint 98510

Leadership When There Is No One to Ask

An Interview with Eni's Franco Bernabè

LINDA HILL AND SUZY WETLAUFER

Executive Summary

FEW CEOS WILL FACE CRISES as disruptive and dramatic as those encountered—and overcome—by Franco Bernabè. In 1992, when Bernabè was appointed CEO of Eni, Italy's large, energy-focused industrial group, his announced goal was to transform the company from a political quagmire into a clean, market-driven business ready for its first public offering. The resistance to his plans was intense, but that wasn't the worst of it. Soon after he took power, an investigation known as *Mani Pulite*—Clean Hands—led to the arrest of much of Eni's senior management team, including the company's chairman. One of those senior managers even made the false claim—based on hearsay—that Bernabè himself had taken a huge bribe.

Simply put, Bernabè's story is not just that of a CEO steering a massive strategic reinvention. It is a story of leadership, and an unlikely one at that.

In this interview, it becomes clear how Bernabè survived his tumultuous first months as CEO and then led the company's transformation. To begin with, he was unique in having both an encyclopedic knowledge of Eni's operations and a view of the company's future from 30,000 feet. But perhaps more than anything, Bernabè's power to lead has come from within. He follows, he says, an inner compass pointed toward humanity and justice. In difficult times, Bernabè seeks consultation from others. But ultimately, he makes all important decisions alone so as not to be buffeted by the needs, emotions, or agendas of others. Such solitude, he believes, is one of the burdens—and necessities—of leadership.

At some point in their careers, most CEOs will lead their organizations through a crisis—a downsizing, for instance, or a merger, or an industrywide upheaval wrought by new technology. But few CEOs will face crises as disruptive and dramatic as those encountered—and overcome—by Franco Bernabè. In his six-year tenure as CEO of Eni, Italy's large, energy-focused industrial group, Bernabè has transformed the organization from a debt-ridden, government-owned, and politically controlled entity into a competitive and profitable publicly traded corporation focused on energy production. He sold off 200 companies, dismissed hundreds of managers, and installed radically new business systems and procedures.

Such changes are not atypical of turnarounds. But at Eni, they occurred under the most daunting circumstances. Several months after Bernabè took power, much of Eni's senior management team was arrested and jailed on corruption charges, and the company's former chairman committed suicide in prison. During the investigations, one of Eni's former managers made the claim that even Bernabè himself had taken a huge bribe. The charge turned out to be based on nothing more than a rumor, but it added to the strain on Bernabè as he worked to revive the company. Simply put, Bernabè's story is not just that of a CEO steering a massive strategic reinvention. It is also one of personal survival—of embracing risk, accepting solitude, and providing strategic and moral direction where little existed. It is a story of leadership, and an unlikely one at that.

When a new government swept into power in Italy in 1992 and appointed Franco Bernabè CEO of Eni, many were shocked. Until then, his nine-year career with the company had been behind the scenes, where he worked as a planner and financial controller. From those positions, Bernabè had developed strategic plans for Eni that were not particularly popular with the company's senior management. In fact, his tireless advocacy for change had prompted the board of directors to demote him once and call for his ouster twice. Yet Bernabè was undeterred, and when he was designated CEO, he made change his top priority. Eni, he announced, would be transformed in short order from a political quagmire into a clean, market-driven business ready for its first public stock offering.

Resistance was quick and intense. Bernabè was regularly excoriated in the media as a traitor or fool who was destined to bring down Eni, with its 135,000 employees and 335 consolidated companies operating in 84 countries. Opponents argued that Eni should not be run like any other company—its mission was national: to ensure Italy's access to energy and to provide jobs.

Further, many believed Eni was so thoroughly entrenched in politics that any attempt to change the system was a waste of time. The government had always appointed many of Eni's managers and directed its strategy, they said, and it always would.

Bernabè believed otherwise. Although he was ostensibly part of a three-man senior leadership team, he sent a directive to the entire company two days after his appointment. Everyone, he announced, would now report to him. While the shock waves were still reverberating, he started replacing hundreds of managers with men and women from lower levels within the company. The new managers not only possessed the technical expertise to move Eni into the future, according to Bernabè, they also shared his vision of Eni's becoming a "typical commercial enterprise" that would be responsive to market needs and shareholder demands. The removal of so many managers was unheard of in a government-owned entity, but the move was even more extraordinary in light of this fact: it was the first time in 30 years that Eni's headquarters had involved itself in the business of the operating units.

Bernabè jumped in with both feet. He directed all operating-company managers to revise their strategic plans to meet Eni's restructuring, value-creation, and performance objectives. Bernabè's deep interest in a disciplined approach to planning met with disbelief and resistance. While beginning to overhaul the company's strategy, Bernabè initiated a campaign to rid Eni of its noncore businesses. Among them was one of the company's few profitable businesses, Nuovo Pignone, a gas turbine and compressor company, which was eventually sold to General Electric. Again, this was a move that shook Eni; besides its financial health, Nuovo

Pignone was well known for its powerful unions. But to the astonishment of many, Bernabè's team negotiated a settlement with the unions.

If matters at Eni weren't difficult enough, they reached the detonating point with Mani Pulite—Clean Hands—an investigation that led to the arrest of some 20 top Eni executives, including chairman Gabriele Cagliari. The investigations were driven by a pervasive mood in the country; Italians wanted their economy wiped clean of embezzlement, bribery, and kickbacks.

The extent of the scandal's impact on Eni caught Bernabè by surprise. Over the years, he had strongly suspected corruption within the upper ranks of the company, he says, but he knew neither its extent nor its mechanisms, or that such a massive degree of personal gain was involved. For instance, he was mortified to learn that one manager stood accused of using embezzled money to buy luxury villas all over Europe. "All of a sudden, I realized how stupid I was," Bernabè recalls. "I was like a parent who did not realize his child was taking drugs. Then, when you find out, you ask, 'How could I not have realized?'"

As Bernabè grappled with this question, prosecutors closed down entire Eni buildings to prevent tampering with evidence; at one point, they shut the company's headquarters in Milan. With a decimated senior-management team, Bernabè worked for weeks almost alone at the top of the company and practically around the clock. He describes the impact of Clean Hands as like "an atomic bomb exploding on your head."

Many Italian companies struck by the Clean Hands investigation claimed their managers were being targeted by mistake. But Bernabè offered no such reassurance. Instead, he asked all the senior managers of Eni's

operating companies for their resignations. He challenged those who remained to see the scandal as he
did: as an opportunity to re-create a more transparent,
productive, and competitive company. The old Eni may
be burning, he told his employees in a speech, but a
new enterprise could rise from its ashes. The transformation would require clarity, transparency, and rigor.

Indeed, Eni has been something of a phoenix in the
years since its crisis. Bernabè's consolidation efforts
have decreased capital spending by $1.3 billion and
debt by $9.1 billion. Labor productivity has risen 112%,
and while revenues have dropped as the company has
divested operations, profits have risen sharply. Eni
posted a loss of $554 million in 1992; in 1997, it
enjoyed profits of $3 billion. And finally, Eni's first public
offering in November 1995 was such a success that the
company held a second tranche in 1996; it sold 1.2
million shares and netted $5.2 billion. The deal was the
largest secondary cash offering in the world and the
largest public offering ever made in Italy. A third
tranche took place in July 1997; in the end, 49% of Eni
was publicly held. The stock, which entered the market
in the $30 range, has recently been trading at more
than $70.

Radical transformations like the one at Eni offer an
opportunity to test common assumptions about leadership. We might assume, for instance, that Franco Bernabè is comfortable with friction and unpredictability.
However, Bernabè actually hates conflict and tries to
avoid it. Nor does he fill the role of the classic charis-
matic leader. He is unprepossessing and shy to the
point of appearing remote. A colleague once
described him as a "surgeon . . . precise, very clear cut,
and on some occasions, without emotions." Bernabè

also defies the model of the leader who has worked his way up the ranks, networking along the way. He began his career as an academic and worked as an economist at Fiat. At Eni, he began as the assistant to the chairman and then worked as the head of planning. He himself will tell you that before being appointed CEO of Eni, he never ran the nitty-gritty of an operating business but worked at the edges—not doing, but listening, observing, and learning.

What then explains Bernabè's power not only to survive Eni's tumultuous transformation but also to lead it? The answer must include his intelligence. He was perhaps one of the few people who could envision Eni as a focused global network of professional businesses; he was able to see the company from 30,000 feet. Yet at the same time, his knowledge of Eni's operations was encyclopedic. Those dual perspectives gave Bernabè the expertise and the credibility to lead the organization through its chaotic transformation.

In another way, Bernabè's leadership is a study in paradox. For nearly ten years, he kept a low profile at Eni and then, when opportunity came knocking, he seized power more boldly than anyone might have expected. A master of exhaustive planning, he is prepared to move swiftly and firmly when necessary, even in the face of enormous risks.

Perhaps more than anything, Bernabè's power to lead comes from within. He follows, he says, an inner compass pointed toward humanity and justice. In difficult times, Bernabè seeks consultation from others. But ultimately, he makes all important decisions alone so as not to be buffeted by the needs, emotions, or agendas of others. Such solitude, he believes, is one of the burdens—and necessities—of leadership.

The source of his inner compass is a topic Bernabè does not discuss easily. He does share, however, a seminal story of his youth. For many years, he spent his weekends volunteering at an institution for elderly people who had no family or financial support. He saw suffering, loneliness, and injustice there, and he became committed to righting such wrongs. At Eni, he discovered that many honest, hard-working employees were having their professional pride stolen by a corrupt minority. And this act of betrayal, he believed, could destroy the whole country.

Bernabè's idealism and patriotism have earned him widespread respect and are perhaps his greatest sources of power. Over the years, people have doubted his strategic goals for Eni, but few have ever questioned his honesty or motives. People widely believe he is a man driven not by personal ambition but by a sincere commitment to the company's and the nation's fate. To this day, most people do not know what Bernabè's political affiliation is—perhaps because he has never had one.

In this interview with Harvard Business School professor Linda Hill and HBR senior editor Suzy Wetlaufer, Bernabè discusses how he handled the challenges he met while leading Eni's transformation, and the new challenges he confronts today.

Eni's troubled period between 1992 and 1995 was once described as an earthquake. Has the ground settled yet?

No, I don't think so. The problems of our organization have been only partially addressed. Back in 1992, we had one objective: to get Eni out of the swamp of politics and corruption. Now our job is to transform the company into something more than a mere multinational. We want to build a great and global company that is able to behave with the agility, creativity, and entrepreneurship that characterize small, aggressive companies.

You have to understand that in its recent history, Eni was told what to do by the government, and its mission was to serve the state. The state wanted an uninterrupted flow of oil, for instance, or it needed jobs created in a particularly poor region of Italy. Eni answered those calls. The company's name had a significant emotional connotation in Italy. It wasn't just another company that people didn't really care about. It represented Italy's postwar reconstruction and modernization. Eni sent a message to the world that Italy was independent and strong, and that no other country would ever control us.

So the Italian people felt as if they owned us, and it followed that the government could direct all our affairs. It worked like this: We had a very complex institutional framework in which ministries and parliamentary committees gave us directives. Everyone wanted a say, everyone had connections within Eni. We had managers around the world, but they thought that their problems were Italian problems, and the solutions had to be looked at in terms of how they would affect Italy.

"I was sick of the political interference. It was destroying the company and it was going to destroy Italy."

As a result, people in the company spent most of their time interpreting the missives of politicians. The politicians wrote documents eight inches thick. And people would pore over them, asking "What did they really mean when they said this or that?" Everyone had his or her own interpretation of what the government wanted Eni to do. You can't imagine the complexity this caused in an organization with 135,000 people and hundreds of companies. But did anyone consider this interpreting a waste of time? No. Not only was it the normal approach to business, it was highly regarded. So you had a company that was very inward-looking. It was really a mess. We had no unique position in the world market; nor did we have a unified strategy.

Today we are a company that answers to its shareholders. We have a strategy and a team in place to execute it. But remember, for 40 years Eni was an important institution within the Italian power system. Some of the attitude that goes along with that legacy remains. We have already undertaken a major cultural revolution, and we have seen excellent results. But the process of cultural change is a continual one, and we still need to aim aggressively at developing a more entrepreneurial attitude within Eni.

You say that Eni still has a long way to go, but in the midst of the crisis, did you ever think that the company would be as competitive and profitable as it is today?

I never lost hope. I knew there was value in the company that could be brought out; I knew Eni had the potential to be great. And I had the motivation to fight. I was sick of the political interference; it was destroying the company and it was going to destroy Italy. There was such injustice, you see.

My basic motivation was moral. Eighty-five percent of the people were paying for the wrongdoings of 15% of the people, who were responsible for the corruption and misuse of politics. They were suffering because that 15% was stealing their professional pride. Their image as good, honest, hard-working people was being stolen from them. I had to right that inequity.

But there were times of terrible stress. Perhaps the worst was when I was charged with taking a bribe. That really destroyed me. It was on television that night, and my children were watching, and they were astonished. I felt like I was at the beginning of a nervous breakdown. It felt so violent—such an act of aggression against me that you cannot imagine. One of the things I have been most careful about in life is my integrity, and here was this person on TV saying, "Bernabè took a $5 million bribe."

I went out, I took a walk. I didn't know how to react at first. But I walked and I thought. When I got back home I said, "This kind of attack is why I am fighting, and I will keep fighting even harder now. And if they think I will go away, they are wrong. Before I am finished, they will all be left behind, the people who think they can control Eni with politics and rumors and lies."

I was very focused, you see, very determined. If I had vacillated about my objectives and my vision for Eni, I would have been finished before I got started. It was really war. It was a question of survival. If I had lost the battle to clean Eni of politics and make it a commercial business, both the company and the country would have suffered. And I truly wanted to save Eni for the young people of Italy, who dreamed as I did.

Now, there were definitely periods when I said, "What am I doing? Why am I standing? Why am I putting this stress on my family? It's too tough, too heavy." But I don't really think I gave serious thought to stopping or quitting. They weren't options because too much was at stake.

When executives lead companies through a crisis, they often don't have time to think; they only have time to react. When Eni was at the height of its troubles, did you reflect on your responsibilities as a leader?

I must say, I did not "react" during the crisis. I always thought things through—I very carefully went through all the problems I had, analyzing them from every angle. Why do you think I walk to work every day? It gives me an extra half hour to think.

Strategic thinking is one of the most critical skills a leader must have. You must view every problem from 360 degrees. You must know your own strengths and weaknesses, as well as those of your organization, your antagonists, and your supporters. Of course, in the midst of a crisis, you often don't have supporters. No one wants to sign up with you until they know you are the winner. So you are alone with the problems, which is for the best. A man I deeply respect, the Israeli leader Shimon Peres, once told me a story. He said that a person knows he is a leader when he realizes there is no one who can answer his questions. He has to answer them himself—alone.

> *"A leader cannot take the weighted average of other people's opinions and make them his own."*

I experienced this sense of being on my own many times during the crisis. I knew I had to answer the questions myself. Therefore I had to reflect on them all patiently and deliberately. You cannot run a large organization superficially. And a leader cannot take the weighted average of other people's opinions and make them his own. You have to organize the information you receive, analyze it, make your decision, and then move on to the next problem. And by doing that, we guided Eni through the crisis.

Let's talk about your story from the beginning. You grew up in Vipiteno, a small northern Italian town, where your father was a railway worker.

Yes, we had a very modest life. My first major experience outside Vipiteno was a trip to the United States as a teenager, when I spent a year there through the American Field Service. It was 1965. I arrived in New York and took a bus across the country to Portland, Oregon. I spoke Italian, German, and French, but knew no English. That trip helped me because I had to resolve problems on my own—very different problems from those I have now, of course, but very important ones for my life. It was good practice.

When I got home, I attended the University of Turin, where I studied political science and economic policy. It was there that I met Franco Reviglio—a renowned economist and one of my professors. Later, when Reviglio went to Eni, I followed him.

But you actually started your career as an academic. In 1975 you edited a book, Financial Structure and Policy in Italy.

Yes, for several years I studied economic theory. Then in 1976 I left Italy for France, where I became a senior economist with the Organization for Economic Cooperation and Development in Paris. When I look back, I see how critical that experience was for my work at Eni. At the OECD, I learned to analyze problems, to get into the details, and to rationalize complex problems by putting them into a clear framework.

But after three years I was restless. I was worried I was becoming a high-level bureaucrat. I did not have

anything more to learn in Paris. So when the chief
economist job at Fiat opened up in 1978, I took it. Here
was an opportunity to apply all that I had learned in my
studies and at the OECD, because Fiat at the time was
trying to change from a very old-fashioned company into
a modern one.

I can look back now and see how important my
training at Fiat was. My time there was during a very
difficult period in Italy. We had terrorism; we had social
upheaval. In the factories there was terrible conflict. We
had almost one casualty every two or three days—people
getting shot or injured. We had strikes almost every day.
Along with many other managers, I was the target of
threats. Being at Fiat—and watching—during this time
helped me learn to deal effectively with conflict and with
complex social, political, and labor problems. And I realized that leaders could make a difference. They could
transform situations that seemed impossible. I mean, at
the time, people thought chaos would overcome business
in Italy.

But as Fiat's restructuring proceeded and tensions
were reduced, I noticed that my job was getting to be like
that of a bureaucrat again. It was becoming dangerously
routine and too specialized. So I went to the head of personnel and said, "I am sick of making macroeconomic
models. Give me something more concrete to do in the
operating divisions." They said, "Look, you're going
nowhere at Fiat. You're doing a good job with your models, but you will never have executive responsibility. So
please go back to your office and give up."

Then in 1983, my old mentor from the University of
Turin, Franco Reviglio, was named chairman of Eni, and
he asked me to come work as his assistant.

Your early years at Eni weren't exactly smooth sailing, either for you or the company.

The company was in terrible shape. It was plagued by an overdiversified portfolio that included oil, newspapers, textiles, metallurgy, and real estate. We had incredible debt, a horrible cost structure, and we were being run by the government. We had no commercial vision whatsoever.

My job was to analyze all the problems that landed on Reviglio's desk. I prepared memos for him explaining the problems, their context, and the implications, and suggested steps that be taken to resolve them. As a result, I spent much of my time studying problems and speaking one-on-one with people in the corporate office who could give me insight into how the company worked. It was solitary work. I visited the operating companies only sporadically and never met with government people or anyone outside of Eni.

"Eni was filled with managers who had the talent to extract the company from the mess it was in."

What I discovered in this period was that Eni was filled with many managers down in the company who had the talent and the desire to extract Eni from the mess it was in. They were engineers and technical experts, really talented professionals, the kind you would find at, say, NASA in the United States. I felt like those people deserved to be liberated from political interference, and I started analyzing every proposal that came across Reviglio's desk from a strictly commercial point of view.

That made me very unpopular with the executive committee. After less than a year, the committee insisted I be removed from my job. But I didn't want to move my family from Rome, and I didn't want to leave Eni. So I bargained with Reviglio for another job in the company. They ended up burying me in the planning department.

Over the following years, you spent your time documenting the steps Eni would have to take to become competitive in a deregulated environment and devising a strategy for privatization. Did anyone pay attention to you?

Reviglio continued to listen to me, and he was very serious about the need to have the company run as a commercial entity. In 1985, I convinced him to renounce the state's endowment fund. That meant Eni would no longer take money from the government to cover its losses. I considered this a great step forward in freeing the company from political influence. Reviglio wanted such freedom, too, but his position required him to engage in complex diplomacy with the government— Eni's only shareholder at the time.

In 1986 the director of planning left, and Reviglio offered me that job. He was in the midst of a great push to restructure Eni, and he wanted me to help. I can't tell you how important this new role was for me. I was able to get a much broader view of the problems facing all our sectors. I could see the company with a 360-degree perspective, how all the parts fit together—or didn't fit. And I got to know the various operating companies like the back of my hand.

At the beginning of the 1990s, pressures on the Italian government to reform increased dramatically. Many people in Italy and throughout Europe saw the need for companies like Eni to rid themselves of political influence. The European economic community demanded that Italy restructure its public finance, which was out of control. As a consequence, the idea of privatization emerged in public and parliamentary debate. But only a few people in the establishment really supported the concept. It was in this context that I was asked to look into the implications of converting Eni into a joint-stock company.

We took the new environment as a sign that we could more openly discuss Eni's problems and how to solve them. We issued a report that said that most of Eni's businesses, with the exception of our big energy companies, AGIP and SNAM, were not adding value and should be divested.

At which point, the board seriously discussed firing you again.

Yes. I was supporting the privatization process too strongly. But I was protected by my peripheral position. I wasn't really in a position to do anything. I was simply making suggestions and writing papers. I didn't have any power.

You suddenly got that power in August of 1992. By then, Reviglio had left the company. Prime Minister Giuliano Amato, a strong supporter of reform and privatization, appointed you CEO of Eni. You were not charged with making Eni a more commercial enterprise but with getting rid of its debt. You were supposed to be leading the company with the chairman and another director who

*was representing the Italian government, but in the
first week, you took control in your first directive to all
the employees. Why?*

Because nothing would have changed. I believed the
government wanted a real change. I had the legal authority to do it, by the way. But normally you don't do something like that without lengthy consultations with the
corporate staff and, of course, with the chairman. But if I
had gone through that process, we would have ended up
with a compromise. I didn't want compromise—I
wanted to have my objectives reached. So I sent the
directive that I was in charge. It was really a shock to the
chairman and everyone else.

There is something to be said for the art of surprise.
And timing is really critical. When a window of opportunity opens, you have to dive through it. You don't see an
open window very often—and when you do, you have to
hope it's not on the top floor! I did not hesitate to dive. I
was ready. I had been studying Eni for almost ten years. I
knew it had the right competencies and the skills down
in the organization. They just had to be brought to the
top of the company.

When I signed my directive, most of the managers
were on summer vacation—in Italy, the whole country
goes away to the beach in August. But that's when I
started working. The directive had been a preemptive
strike, really, to set the stage for all my subsequent
actions. I spent the month studying our operating companies; there were 176 of them in Italy and 159 abroad. I
didn't hold formal meetings. Instead, I walked around
and spoke one-on-one with the executives and middle
managers who had not gone away on vacation. I told
them of my plans for the company's privatization. Most
were shocked, first, that I was even there and, second,

that I would get involved in their business and actually cared to hear their opinions. They were used to being told what to do. But I also found that many of them were intrigued by my free-market orientation.

I was also struck by how hard it was going to be to reach my dream. Reality hit me in the face. Although data for making projections existed, the information was not in a useful form. Furthermore, the information systems the company had in place were archaic. And, of course, there were no data on competitors or markets to speak of. Eni had the mentality of a public utility.

When everyone returned in September from their vacations, I picked up the pace. I insisted that executives prepare strategic plans for my review that would reflect the restructuring required by privatization. And I began to move managers around. At some of the worst-performing companies, I replaced whole management teams. People thought I was crazy. They said, "You can't do this without political approval." I told them the changes were strictly commercial; I wasn't planning on consulting anyone in the government about who was going to run the businesses.

That was the beginning of a period of civil war within Eni. I wanted Eni to go on the stock market as an integrated company; that was well known. In September, the chairman of AGIP, our upstream subsidiary that produces oil and is one of our major profit centers, went to the press and told them he was going to float AGIP's stock separately. In November came our annual meeting, at which the operating company executives were supposed to present their four-year plans. Remember, I had directed them to draw up plans that would reflect the privatization program. None of them had. Not a single one. So I stood up and told them all that their plans were unacceptable. There was total silence.

I continued. I presented my four-year strategic plan, which gave explicit guidelines for restructuring Eni. The executives in the room looked at me as if I were from the moon. Very few of them believed I was going to be around long enough to make them do anything. They ignored what I asked for, and more than that, many of them were actively fighting against me, against privatization—against everything!

It was in the midst of this civil war that the Clean Hands investigation erupted. About two dozen of Eni's executives were charged, including the company's chairman.

Yes, everything started collapsing. Many people in the company wanted reassurance from me that we would overcome the mess and that everyone would come out clean. They wanted to hear that it was some kind of mistake. I knew that saying those words would have boosted morale, given people confidence, and generally made the whole process easier. Other Italian companies were using this approach. They said, "Nothing is wrong. It is a judicial mistake. We are all free of guilt." I made the opposite choice. I asked all those accused to resign, and I went even further. I asked for the resignation of every senior manager in all of Eni's operating companies.

I realized I had to rebuild from the grass roots. I wanted to have a new, green field on which to rebuild the company. If I had simply fired those who had been arrested, I would have implicitly accused them without a fair trial. So, without accusing anyone, I asked them all to resign. When they protested I was able to say, "I am not accusing you of anything. I want the freedom to remotivate and reorganize the company."

It was a very difficult decision for me from both a psychological and a managerial perspective. I could not judge the guilt or innocence of the people arrested. And replacing all the senior managers would mean putting Eni in the hands of men and women who were untested—people who had never had the chance to run a big company before. But I did it anyway. Nobody wanted things to go on as before. It was a big risk, but it was also a big opportunity. In less than two months, I replaced more than 250 senior managers.

I gave a speech to the employees to explain what I was doing. I wanted people to understand that my changes were part of the great transformation of Italy into a modern country. The crisis we were in was a result of an unsustainable system in which companies were asked to answer to two masters: the state and the bottom line. The old patronage system was based on political appointments, and the rules of the game too often disregarded professionalism, merit, experience, and results. Change would be painful, but it would put Eni at the forefront of a radical and necessary modernization of our country.

Of course, the attacks from people in the government and from other opponents continued. And some of the managers who remained at Eni still fought me. In 1993, the prime minister who had appointed me left office. Some people thought I too might be removed from my position, but officials in the government were having so many of their own problems, they didn't come looking for me.

How did you fill the empty executive positions? Did you turn to outsiders?

I took the exact opposite approach. With the head of HR, I pored over hundreds of résumés from people within Eni. A lot of people—consultants and investment bankers—told me to look outside the company. But I believed there was plenty of talent inside the company that only needed to be nurtured and given the right tools to succeed. We would choose people according to their experience and performance.

I wanted them to be professionally sound, naturally, but that was the easy part. More difficult was finding people who would give me guarantees of integrity and show signs of independence. One person I chose, for instance, had once left Eni because he found the company too bureaucratic and cumbersome. I asked him to become CFO. You see, I wanted people I could count on in a real battle, because the war to transform Eni into a true commercial enterprise was not yet over.

I finally got a team in place to move forward toward privatization. It was hard work. We had existing systems for information management, capital budgeting, operations planning, and strategic planning, but they were inadequate. As a consequence, we had to create a completely new set of rules, processes, and procedures. And we had to create our first code of practice. (See "Transparency and Honesty: The Eni Code" at the end of this article.)

"A person who has to make important decisions has to make them alone. You need an inner compass to indicate the way."

In my early years as CEO, we had to review every process. Every single one. And so we created manuals for everything—the disposal of assets, for instance. Up to that point, people bought things at Eni but never sold them. We had to create a process for selling assets, and we had to codify it. Creating the manuals was labor intensive, to put it mildly, but we were building a new Eni, and it had to be done. And this effort helped psychologically, too, because people felt overwhelmed, and the manuals walked them through every action. When results started coming, people saw the purpose of all the planning.

You're calm as you describe these events. Were you calm when you were going through them?

I would say so. I was tired, of course, and sometimes very worried. But if I had become emotional, no one would have benefited. I think this is one of the main lessons I have learned. When you are in a position like mine, you can never be driven by your emotions. That doesn't mean you shouldn't get to know other people and listen to their feelings. Indeed, listening is critical for getting anything done. If you need another person to see your point of view—to come to your side in a matter such as privatization—then you need to learn his or her motivations. But you cannot let that person's emotions sway you.

A person who has to make important decisions has to make them alone. You can rely on no one. In Italian, we call this condition *solitudine*. If you are in a difficult situation, as I was for a long time, then it can be very dangerous to listen too much to others or to depend on them. You have to watch every bit of the picture. And then you need an inner compass to indicate the way. In my case, that compass was my conscience. If I had discussed the pros and cons of my decisions with other people or tried to balance the risks, my compass would have been thrown off. Such discussions would have gotten in the way of what I knew was the right thing to do. The right thing to do was to pull the company out of the swamp of politics that it was mired in. My compass told me where to go and what I needed to do to get there.

When you are part of the crowd, you have an entirely different feeling from when you are apart from it. The more responsibility you have, the more you need to be alone.

Along with your inner compass, what else accounts for your success in leading Eni's transformation?

I had a sense of strategic direction. When your company is collapsing, people rarely have that sense. I did. Many people around me had political objectives, power objectives. Finally, people started to follow me because, even if they didn't like me or agree with me, they saw I was determined, and they took some comfort in following me. They said, "Well, let's see where he takes us."

You see, I had a clear objective—and having one will allow you to surmount whatever difficulty you have when you start something that seems impossible. Believe me, when we started talking about privatization, everyone said it could never be done. They said our legal problems and our logistical problems were insurmountable.

There are so many companies where the leaders speak in management talk when they face difficulties—they use incomprehensible formulas, they say what they want to do in excruciating detail, and so on and so forth. In our case, the objective was very clear: we wanted the company privatized.

The very detailed planning helped. The plans pushed us forward even when we felt as if we were stalled. There is a point when you start feeling that nothing is getting done because there are so many things to do. The process is so big and complex; it feels overwhelming. And then you see some detailed action plan, and you follow it. Sometimes putting one foot in front of the other is the only way to make a huge change.

And finally, communication. I think this is one of the most critical factors for success in changing a big organization. I had to learn as CEO how to communicate. I was used to writing articles and preparing reports, but those are not really very effective communication tools. People can fall asleep after two minutes of reading. And you can talk to five senior managers around a table, but you find a month later that no one in the second or third levels of the organization knows you or your objectives.

I realized the most effective thing to do was give speeches to large groups within the organization. I try to give one a month. You can reach so many people, so many levels of the organization. But a speech can be like an article if you're not careful. So the speech has to have emotional content. To be effective, you have to tap into people's sentiments, feelings, and emotions.

And your message has to be simple. You can't imagine how distorted a message can get when it is passed along thirdhand. The only way to combat this noise in the transmission is to communicate directly with everyone involved and to make simple points. That requires enormous patience, but it is the only way.

Would you say, then, that leadership is about setting objectives, planning, and communicating?

All those things, yes, but leadership is fundamentally about humanity. It is about morality. Your primary job as a leader is to see what is good for your organization and what is good for the people who work for you, and to create something for the well-being of your fellow citizens. This is why I was driven to right the injustice afflicting Eni: to help the good people in Eni and in Italy who didn't deserve to suffer for the wrongdoings of the few.

When I think about great leadership, I often think of what Franklin Roosevelt did in March 1941, when he went before Congress seeking support for Great Britain in its fight against the Nazis. Many Americans opposed him. "Keep out of the war," they said. But he believed it was right to come to Britain's aid. The country was desperate. Roosevelt reminded America that you do not ask your neighbors to pay you for a fire extinguisher when their house is on fire. And he convinced the vast majority. This was the turning point of the war. And I would say the entire history of the century would have come out differently if Roosevelt had not done what was right not just for the United States but for humankind.

Leadership requires a willingness to take risks. I took many big risks. But I had two psychological parachutes. First, I was young enough that being fired for pursuing the right ideas wouldn't hurt me—it would be to my credit. I could have worked somewhere else. Second, I never used the paraphernalia of the position. Being the chief executive of a company like Eni, and one of the top managers in the country, you have offered to you a number of perks that can make your life different. I didn't take them. I lived in the same house in which I was living before; I drove the same car. I didn't change my behavior. I still walked to work, and I didn't start going to lunches and dinners and taking on a big social life. I remained exactly as I was. If I had lost my job and gone back to something more subdued and less glamorous—well, it wouldn't have changed my life. So taking risks didn't seem that frightening to me. I didn't have anything to lose.

You've said your next challenge for Eni is to transform its culture. Is that your main goal now?

It's one of the them. I would like to create a company of entrepreneurs—a company that is so free of bureaucracy that all that is left are people who create value. And we have other strategic challenges. We need to focus on the business of the core group, for instance.

Those goals are critical, but I've found that the most important things I think about now are the immaterial ones. The things you can't touch or feel, the problems that no one else can answer. I spend much of my time reading. I read reports from my staff, or course, but I also read literature, history, and philosophy.

On the subject of strategy, I have just read *The Art of War*, the classic text written some 2,500 years ago by the Chinese general Sun Tzu. It's the first comprehensive text on strategy that can still be applied to all kinds of human activity. Some of his observations remind me of chess. You know, more or less, how to react when you play with an opponent at your level. But when you play with someone who is relatively new to the game, you may end up losing because his moves are so unpredictable. And I think the best book about leadership is a novel, *Memoirs of Hadrian*, by the French writer Marguerite Yourcenar. In this book, you come to see why Hadrian was one of the greatest Roman emperors. He did not have sophisticated training or leadership experience, but he did have a good understanding of human nature, and he was able to draw out the best from everybody. That is leadership.

Ideas and information are very important to you. Do you spend a lot of time in meetings?

We don't have a lot of meetings at Eni. These days, I see each of my direct reports several times a week, and I read documents prepared for me so that I can understand Eni's problems clearly and from every perspective.

I don't deal with all of Eni's problems, of course. What I must deal with are the intangible things, the most frustrating problems. Most people want to deal with practical things. How do I handle my account? How do I conceive the advertising campaign? How do I build this particular technology? People want to work on something that is concrete, something that they can touch. What's left behind is my work.

I have been thinking lately about how Eni should approach information technology. Usually CEOs don't deal with this; they leave it to the chief information officer. But I was thinking about laptops and how Eni would use them. The head of a computer company asked me, "Why are you wasting your time thinking about the capabilities of your laptop? You're the CEO." And I told him that understanding how a laptop worked was part of my job in creating Eni's culture. How should people in our organization connect with one another? What could be more important than finding the answer to that question?

Imagine it's ten years from now—2008. What does Eni look like, and are you its CEO?

I don't know if I will be its CEO. But I do know that when you want to transform a company of this size, it takes much longer than the time I have behind my shoulders. It's been only six years.

When you are trying to change a company, everyone wants to see quick results. Which is odd, because people also resist change so much. People don't like risk, they don't like adventure—it doesn't make any difference where you work. When you push through change, people first oppose you, then they become angry, then sad and desperate, and then they more or less have a nervous breakdown. No one ever sees the value of change while it is happening. Meanwhile, you have the management books telling you that big change initiatives need quick wins. In reality, it takes patience and time.

Eni has come a long way, it's true. In 1992, our business was not focused and we were controlled by the state. Today we are much, much leaner, no longer corrupt, and liberated from political influence. We are the fifth-most-profitable publicly traded oil company in the world, which is remarkable when you consider that we are located in a country that has no natural supply of hydrocarbons. But when I think of where I want to bring Eni, I still have a great deal of work to do. What I have in mind is transforming a big oil corporation into a professional organization like a law firm, in which everyone is a partner and an entrepreneur who creates value for the organization.

There is always so much to do before one retires. You can transform an organization many times.

Transparency and Honesty: The Eni Code

OF ALL HIS ACCOMPLISHMENTS at Eni, Franco Bernabè counts his stewardship of the company's first-ever code of practice among the most meaningful. The code has two purposes. First, it articulates the rigorous business practices and policies of the new Eni. Second, it makes those practices and policies transparent to the world.

The Transformation of Eni, 1992–1998

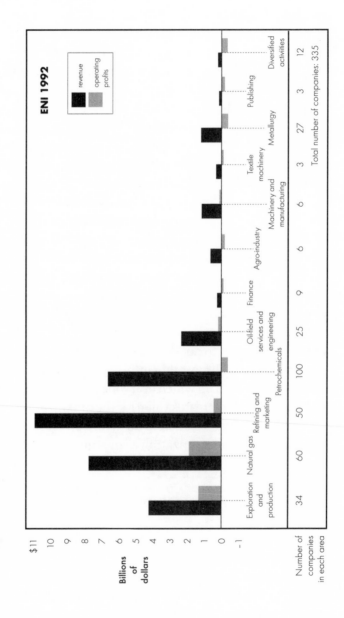

ENI 1992

Legend:
- revenue
- operating profits

Billions of dollars: $11, 10, 9, 8, 7, 6, 5, 4, 3, 2, 1, 0, -1

Categories:
- Exploration and production
- Natural gas
- Refining and marketing
- Petrochemicals
- Oilfield services and engineering
- Finance
- Agro-industry
- Machinery and manufacturing
- Textile machinery
- Metallurgy
- Publishing
- Diversified activities

Number of companies in each area	34	60	50	100	25	9	6	6	3	27	3	12

Total number of companies: 335

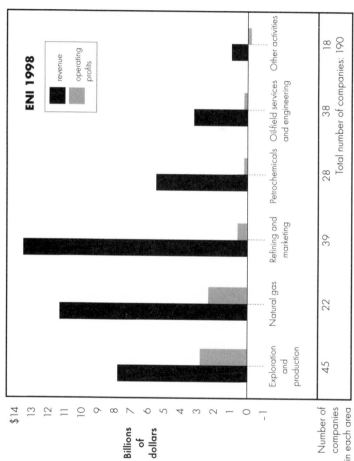

ENI 1998

Legend:
- revenue
- operating profits

Billions of dollars

| $14 |
| 13 |
| 12 |
| 11 |
| 10 |
| 9 |
| 8 |
| 7 |
| 6 |
| 5 |
| 4 |
| 3 |
| 2 |
| 1 |
| 0 |
| −1 |

	Exploration and production	Natural gas	Refining and marketing	Petrochemicals	Oil-field services and engineering	Other activities
Number of companies in each area	45	22	39	28	38	18

Total number of companies: 190

In 1992, when Franco Bernabè was appointed CEO of Eni, the company was struggling in disarray. Plagued by a wildly diversified portfolio ranging from oil to newspapers, it was also drowning in debt. Overall, the company consisted of 335 operating companies, and almost all of them were losing money.

Today Eni consists of five main businesses revolving around energy production. More significant, perhaps, is the fact that the company will end 1997 with an operating profit of $3 billion. Indeed, it is the fifth-most-profitable publicly traded oil company in the world, a result made especially notable given that Italy has no natural supply of hydrocarbons.

Below is a timeline that highlights some of the extraordinary political, social, and strategic events that took place as Bernabè transformed Eni.

1992

August: Franco Bernabè is appointed CEO of Eni.

August: Bernabè issues his first directive, stating that "after today, everyone reports directly to me."

September: As a first step in fighting the company's financial crisis, Bernabè begins removing dozens of top-level and midlevel managers.

1993

February: Italy's Clean Hands investigation begins.

March: Top Eni executives are arrested on corruption charges.

April: Bernabè asks all the senior managers of Eni's operating companies to resign.

July: Eni's ex-chairman, Gabriele Cagliari, commits suicide in jail.

November: To date, 30 operating companies have been sold, and negotiations on the sale of 50 more are in process.

December: Bernabè is accused by a former Eni manager of taking a $5 million bribe.

December: Nuovo Pignone is sold to General Electric.

1994

January: Eni's code of practice, a response to the Clean Hands crisis, is developed, approved by Bernabè and the board of directors, and distributed to all Eni employees.

July: Some political parties begin to call for Bernabè's resignation.

August: By now, 57 subsidiaries have been sold, and 43 more sales are projected by the year's end.

1995	1996	1997	1998

1995

August: The Italian government appoints a global advisor for Eni's privatization, a decisive step in moving the process forward.

November: The first tranche of the initial public offering is launched. The sale raises more than $4 billion for the Italian treasury.

December: More than 120 companies and business activities have been sold, and an equal number have been closed down.

1996

October: A second tranche is launched: a public offering of 1.2 million shares. This sale lowers government ownership of Eni to 69%.

1997

July: The third public offering of shares is completed. It lowers government interest in Eni to just over 51%.

December: About 230 companies and business activities have been sold since Bernabè became CEO.

1998

A fourth tranche of Eni shares is expected this year that will decrease the state-owned percentage of the company to below 50%.

Bernabè personally supervised the preparation of the code, which was approved by Eni's board of directors in January 1994. Today it is company policy that every employee be given a copy of the code, and most executives display it proudly on their desks.

The excerpts below may not sound too different from other corporate codes, but for Eni the code broke new ground. In laying out company values and standards of behavior, as well as explicitly identifying and forbidding conflicts of interest, the code sent a signal that business at Eni would never again be anything but honorable.

The prime responsibility of employees is to be good, law-abiding citizens, striving for the Eni Group's success in a spirit of fair competition.

Being a part of the Eni Group . . . means respecting company rules and adhering to the values of professionalism, transparency, and honesty.

All the activities within the company must be carried out with professional commitment and ethical rigor. All employees must contribute professionally in accordance with their responsibilities, and they must act in such a way as to protect the company's image. Relations among employees at all levels must reflect honesty, loyalty, and mutual respect. No employee shall make improper use of the assets and resources of Eni or allow anyone else to do so.

It is primarily up to supervisors to see that the values and principles contained in the code are respected, to carry out their responsibilities both internally and externally, and to strengthen confidence, a sense of cohesion, and group spirit. Management is required to propose and implement projects, actions, and investments designed to increase the long-term value of the company's financial, managerial, and technological assets, the return to share-holders, the long-term well-being of employees, and the community.

Originally published in July–August 1998
Reprint 98402

Lincoln Electric's Harsh Lessons from International Expansion

DONALD F. HASTINGS

Executive Summary

LESS THAN HALF AN HOUR after Donald Hastings became chairman and CEO of the Lincoln Electric Company in July 1992, he got the shocking news: losses from the company's European operations were so steep that Lincoln was at risk of defaulting on its loans and being unable to pay its employees their year-end bonus. Since the bonus was the foundation of the company's unusually successful manufacturing operations, Hastings knew that failure to pay it could lead to the company's unraveling.

How had Lincoln gotten into this predicament? By a program of rapid foreign expansion. Lincoln was primarily a U.S. company until the mid-1980s, but recession at home and competition from abroad led executives to dream that the company could become a global power.

Between 1986 and 1991, Lincoln took on unprecedented debt in order to finance foreign acquisitions, mostly in Europe. A number of factors doomed the venture: recession in Europe, unfamiliarity with Europe's labor culture, lack of international expertise at the top. But the root cause, Hastings admits, was overconfidence on the part of Lincoln's leaders in the company's manufacturing abilities and systems.

Hastings, now chairman emeritus, recounts how the company suffered through the early 1990s and then returned to prosperity. It wrote off most of its European operations, ramped up domestic production and sales, and hired top managers and board members with international experience. As a result of strenuous efforts at all levels of the company, it managed to keep paying the bonus and to largely regain the trust of its people.

AT 5:01 P.M. ON THE LAST FRIDAY OF JULY 1992, I took over as chairman and CEO of the Lincoln Electric Company. I had worked at Lincoln for 38 years and had reached the pinnacle of my career. But my exhilaration lasted exactly 24 minutes.

At 5:25 P.M., while I was engaged in small talk in the hallway, Ellis Smolik, our chief financial officer, walked up and said, "I've got some grim news. The numbers just came in from the European operations, and they're bad. Very bad. They lost almost $7.5 million in June, and that means we'll have to report a second quarter loss. We'll violate our covenants with the banks and default on our loans."

Driving home an hour and a half later, I agonized over what I had just learned. The profits from our main operations in the United States wouldn't be enough to offset our losses abroad. And while Europe was our biggest problem, we also were losing money in Latin America and Japan. We would have to report a consolidated loss of $12 million for the quarter. In the 97-year history of the company, we had never experienced a consolidated loss. I could imagine the headline in the local newspaper: "New CEO at Lincoln Electric Fumbles in First 24 Minutes on the Job." It was a horrible night for me. I got very little sleep. In fact, it would be almost two years before I would have a good night's rest.

During the next week, I confirmed the magnitude of the crisis through conversations with our managers in Europe and our international people at home. When I asked them whether they might be able to turn around their businesses quickly, they were pessimistic—the third quarter in Europe is traditionally the weakest due to shutdowns for vacations and holidays. They expected even poorer results. In addition, there was no indication that our problems in Latin America and Japan were going to diminish. Our financial situation was clearly going to get a lot worse.

My thoughts raced ahead to December, when we were scheduled to pay out the annual incentive bonus to our U.S. workforce. Despite a soft economy, our operations in the United States had done well. Our 3,000 U.S. workers would expect to receive, as a group, more than $50 million. If we were in default, we might not be able to pay them. But if we didn't pay the bonus, the whole company might unravel.

To understand why the bonus is so important, you have to understand a few things about the company. Lincoln Electric was founded by John C. Lincoln in 1895, and manufacturing has been its heart and soul. For decades, the company has been one of the leading manufacturers of arc-welding products in the world. At the end of World War II, more than 50 manufacturers of arc-welding products competed in the United States; today only six major manufacturers remain. The vast majority, including such corporate giants as General Electric and Westinghouse, withdrew from the business primarily because Lincoln sold high-value, high-quality products at competitive prices and with outstanding customer service.

The company also makes industrial electric motors, but arc-welding products are the mainstay business. In 1992, they accounted for more than 87% of our $853 million in total sales. Lincoln then had a leading 40% of the domestic market for electrodes and welding wires, the consumables that constitute the heart of the business, and it was neck and neck with Miller Electric Manufacturing of Appleton, Wisconsin, for the lead in machines.

Lincoln's incentive system, which combines a bonus with piecework—the practice of paying each factory worker on the basis of how many units he or she produces instead of hourly wages or salaries—is an integral part of the company's culture. The system has long distinguished Lincoln from other U.S. companies and has been the subject of a popular case study at Harvard Business School. Historically, bonuses have constituted more than 50% of our U.S. employees' annual incomes. And the system has allowed those people to rank among the highest paid factory workers in the world. Hundreds of them have earned $70,000 to $80,000 in a year, and several handfuls have made more than $100,000.

The incentive system was created in 1934, and bonuses had been paid every year since then. To someone like me who was raised at Lincoln—I joined the company as a sales trainee in 1953, shortly after graduating from Harvard Business School—not paying the bonus was unimaginable.

The Rush to Globalize

How had we gotten into this predicament? By a program of rapid foreign expansion. Although Lincoln had had manufacturing and marketing operations in Canada, Australia, and France for more than 40 years, all three were independent of one another and were treated like colonies. Lincoln was primarily a U.S. company, and its two main plants were—and still are—in the Cleveland area. It was our more recent, much bigger ventures overseas that got us into trouble.

Since the deep U.S. recession of the early 1980s, we had been talking about expanding abroad so that we wouldn't be so dependent on the domestic market. But William Irrgang, who headed Lincoln from 1965 until 1986, adamantly opposed the idea. Then in 1986, Bill Irrgang died and was succeeded by George E. "Ted" Willis, and I was named president of North American operations.

Ted dreamed of Lincoln's becoming a global power. He immediately purchased Harris Calorific, a manufacturer of oxyfuel cutting equipment that had plants in Italy and the United Kingdom. At that time, we also got a sharp wake-up call from the market when ESAB, a major manufacturer of arc-welding products based in Sweden, suddenly bought two midsize manufacturers in the United States. ESAB, which was already operating in the Far East and Latin America, obviously had global ambitions. We feared further incursions on the U.S. market by

ESAB, which would be able to use its non-U.S. profits to buy market share. But we could not buy domestic competitors ourselves because of antitrust laws. So we decided to take the battle to ESAB's markets in Europe and Latin America. Our response would have to be quick—and substantial.

During the next five years of the Willis regime, we spent almost $325 million on expansion, a huge sum for a company of our size. We built three greenfield plants in Japan, Venezuela, and Brazil and purchased operations with eight plants in Germany, Norway, the United Kingdom, the Netherlands, Spain, and Mexico. Many of those acquisitions were made at the peak of their market cycles and cost top dollar. For example, we bought an operation in Barcelona just after the 1988 Olympics, when the Spanish economy was booming and the construction market was incredibly strong. In less than a year, the Spanish economy fell into a deep recession.

Ted made the acquisition decisions, took charge of the negotiations, and required all the new foreign operations, with the exception of those in Canada and Mexico, to report directly to him. Of our board's 15 directors, 12 were insiders—current and former Lincoln executives and members of the founding family. None of us had any significant international experience. No one on the board, including me, ever seriously challenged Ted. We believed that because we were so successful in the United States, we could be successful anywhere.

Without truly exploring the idea, we assumed that the incentive system would be accepted abroad.

In fact, when we examined the manufacturing operations of the foreign companies on our acquisition list, we saw tremendous opportunities to reduce costs by applying our manufacturing expertise, equipment, and incentive system. We also knew that we could not afford to export consumables, namely certain electrodes and wire, from the United States. That was and still is a cutthroat commodity business; had we exported those items, the shipping costs and duties would have prohibited us from being price competitive.

But we also made several mistaken assumptions. For example, without truly exploring the idea, we assumed that the incentive system would be accepted abroad. We found, however, that the European culture of labor was hostile to the piecework and bonus system.

In addition, we concluded that we could not export arc-welding machines to many European countries, especially Germany, the major market in Europe. Our distributors, along with our French and Norwegian managers, told us repeatedly they could not sell products designed and manufactured in the United States to Europeans because of their bias toward their own goods. The managers insisted that it was impossible to establish a foothold in Germany unless we bought an established local player. Unfortunately, we listened well, accepted their assertions, and then acted on them—without testing them.

In April 1991 we concluded our largest acquisition: certain assets of Germany's Messer Griesheim, including a plant that manufactured arc-welding machines, at a cost of more than $70 million. At the time, we were counting on the German economy to remain strong. We did not foresee the consequences of German reunification. The government's huge outlays to rebuild eastern Germany led the inflation-wary Bundesbank to raise interest rates, one of several events that triggered the deepest recession in Europe since World War II.

After the Messer acquisition, Ted assigned John Gonzalez, vice president of engineering, the job of managing the European factories. John had no international experience and was not expected to focus on sales or marketing. Indeed, some of the European managing directors continued to report directly to Ted. It is doubtful that John ever really wanted the assignment; he never relocated to Europe. In early 1992 he gave up the responsibility and returned to Cleveland to head our R&D efforts.

In hindsight, I realize that John's appointment reflected a broader problem: our corporate management lacked sufficient international expertise and had little experience running a complex, dispersed organization. Our managers didn't know how to run foreign operations; nor did they understand foreign cultures. Consequently, we had to rely on people in our foreign companies—people we didn't know and who didn't know us.

Ted turned next to Rolf Jonassen, the head and former co-owner of Norweld—a Norwegian company with factories in Norway, the United Kingdom, and the Netherlands—which we had acquired before our purchase of Messer Griesheim. Rolf was named to lead the management company that we set up to run Lincoln's European operations. With his experience running a multinational, he seemed like a solid choice. He reported directly to Ted.

My own involvement in the international arena was minimal at this point. As president, the only foreign operations that reported to me were the ones in Canada and Mexico. And before becoming president, my responsibility as vice president of sales for 15 years was limited to the United States.

As a director and as president, I did see the budgets and financial reports submitted by our foreign operations. By 1991 none of them, with the exception of those in Canada and Australia, were performing well. (Profits had often been elusive at our French operation, which should have stood as a warning about global expansion.) The operation in Brazil had been a sinkhole from the beginning, and the operations in Germany, Japan, Mexico, and Venezuela had never made money. The rest were marginally profitable when we bought them, although none had world-class factories. Our manufacturing expertise and systems could easily bring them up to that standard, we thought.

Warning Signs

For more than a year before becoming CEO, however, I witnessed a troubling pattern. The individual European businesses would submit extremely optimistic sales and profits targets in their budgets. But they invariably missed the targets—often by quite a bit—and the gaps were getting bigger and bigger. Even more worrisome, nobody seemed to have a handle on why the targets were being missed or what to do about the gaps. When asked, the businesses' managers would say, "We were too optimistic. The recession is worse than we thought. We'll downsize the budget." There was absolutely no fire in their bellies to correct the problem of declining sales.

In April 1991 the board informed me that the top job would be mine at the end of July 1992. My unease about Europe was deepening, but Ted did not seem unduly worried. He did, however, have me take two short trips to Europe in late 1991 and early 1992. I was aghast at the managers' lack of concern about the need to boost revenues. They seemed perfectly content to just ride out the recession.

Understandably, given Lincoln's history, Ted looked at the situation primarily from a manufacturing standpoint. He was a brilliant engineer and manufacturing executive. All four of my predecessors as Lincoln's chairman had engineering and manufacturing backgrounds, and all four were of the firm belief that if you had the lowest-cost, highest-quality manufacturing operation, you would automatically dominate the market.

With my background in sales and marketing, I knew that quality, low-cost manufacturing would not be enough. Having a stellar manufacturing operation and a good product is a wonderful advantage. But if you don't have proper distribution, competitive delivery times, relationships in the marketplace, and people who can understand and help customers, you won't succeed.

Ted operated very much on his own. Part of the reason for that was his personality, but part of it was the company's heritage. Ted's predecessors had handled an enormous amount by themselves. Everything of importance went directly to the CEO.

Our second chairman, James F. Lincoln, the founder's brother and the company's leader from 1929 until 1965, once wrote that no company should ever grow larger than one man could administer or manage. We exceeded that size even before we began the foreign expansion, but it took the crisis to make us realize that we had reached the limits of the management approaches and skills that had served us so well when we were a smaller, simpler company.

When it became clear that Ted was primarily focused on improving the worldwide manufacturing operations by increasing efficiency and reducing costs, I decided to take my concerns to the board's nominating committee. I asked that the succession be accelerated and that I be given responsibility for Europe—I would use my sales and marketing background to increase revenues. "We should make a change," I said. But out of deference to Ted, the committee said, "No, you've got to wait until next year."

With the onset of the recession in 1992, the European operations began to deteriorate rapidly. The numbers reported in May and June were not good—the profits were marginal—and then came the awful news in July. The magnitude of the second quarter loss caught everyone by surprise. Even I, who'd been openly worried, never imagined that the losses would be big enough to throw the entire company into the red.

What we had not fully considered was that the very fact of borrowing would be a major cultural shock to our employees.

Although Ted knew that the foreign operations were in trouble, he continued to be outwardly optimistic. He was confident that Lincoln's manufacturing prowess would enable us to make a success of the foreign operations.

Ted had tried to help the sales forces in Europe in October 1991: he sent Jim Clauson, our New England regional manager, overseas to teach them sales and marketing techniques that were successful in the United States. But Jim was rebuffed by his European counterparts. It would take CEO status—on-site—to catch their attention.

Should We Pay the Bonus? Could We?

Lincoln had always been ultraconservative financially. Before making the acquisitions, we had a cash reserve of more than $70 million and no debt. By 1990 we had used up that surplus and taken on a small amount of debt. In 1992 our debt soared to nearly $250 million, or 63% of equity.

Our directors—myself included—had known that Lincoln would have to borrow to finance the acquisitions. What we had not fully considered, however, was that the very fact of borrowing would be a major cultural shock to our employees. Most people at Lincoln saw the taking on of *any* debt as reckless, a view that had its roots in our incentive system. Ever since the bonus was introduced, management had explained to employees that it was a cash-sharing rather than a profit-sharing bonus. First we had to use the company's profits to take care of our shareholders with dividends and to invest in Lincoln's future. Only after those needs were met could we pay the bonus. If there was no cash left, there would be no bonus.

As soon as it became apparent that we were going to have to borrow to finance the foreign expansion, employees became concerned. They could see it affecting their incomes. And, as our level of debt increased, they grew deeply worried—and they let senior managers know it.

Lincoln has long preached and practiced open communication. Any employee who feels the need to speak to the CEO can see him. And many do. The same holds true for other Lincoln executives; all have open doors. In this instance, employees—individually and through our 29-member employee advisory board—made their fears known. "How can there be a cash bonus if we don't have any cash that's ours?" people repeatedly asked our executives.

After taking over as CEO, I was faced with a terrible predicament. We could pay the bonus by taking the company deeper into debt. Or we could announce that there would be no bonus and lose our people's trust—hence sacrificing the company's long-term competitive edge.

Except for the workers at the newly acquired Harris Calorific, all our U.S. employees were eligible for a bonus. Rank-and-file factory workers were graded twice during the year on four types of performance: the quality of their work, the quantity of their work, their dependability, and their cooperation. The first two ratings motivated workers to do their individual best. If the grading stopped there, we probably would have had chaos; everyone would have been out for himself. The last two ratings encouraged people to work together and contribute ideas that would help everyone.

Because of the bonus and piecework pay, employees at our Cleveland-area factories and in our sales, distribution, and customer service centers throughout the United States act like entrepreneurs. The bonus is payment for outstanding performance. Lincoln employees do perform—and not just in terms of high productivity and quality. Absentee and turnover rates historically are very low. In 1992 absentee rates were between 1.5% and 2%, and the turnover rate, including retirement but excluding new employees (people employed for 90 days or less), was 3.5%. When we have severe snowstorms, most of Cleveland shuts down, but Lincoln people make it in.

Because our system draws out the best in people, they don't require much supervision. The foreman-to-worker ratio at Lincoln's main U.S. plants is 1 to 100. In a typical factory in the United States, the ratio is 1 to 25; in some auto assembly plants, it is 1 to 10. The savings from having relatively few supervisors helps the company pay the bonus. It was clear to me at the time that if we dropped the bonus, we would have to hire more employees because our productivity would go down. In other words, we couldn't try to save money by cutting out the bonus.

In the second week of August 1992, we got a break. Harry Carlson, the company's vice chairman, met with two major Cleveland banks: National City Bank and Key Bank. They wanted to help. They immediately agreed to relax the covenants, provided that we seek a higher line of credit with a larger group of banks. They even promised to help us negotiate a new line of credit. One worry had been alleviated: we would be able to pay the bonus.

Still Bleeding in Europe

That same week I left for Europe. I had no choice, even though I lacked extensive international experience. None of the other senior managers had any either. The CFO, Ellis Smolik, who joined me on the trip, didn't even have a passport; we had to scramble to get him one at the last minute.

During the next 11 months, I would go to Europe twice a month on average, staying from seven to ten days at a time. My first priority that August was to meet with all the European managing directors and their sales managers. I assigned them the job of developing plans, complete with detailed sales strategies, for turning around their businesses. The plans were to cover the fourth quarter of 1992 and all of 1993. The goal was to create profitable operations in 1993. The managing directors—along with our other foreign directors—were asked to submit their plans by early October.

In October we brought in Orin Schaeffer, the former CFO of Goodyear, as a consultant. Schaeffer, who had international financial experience, worked with J.P.

Morgan to put together a ten-bank consortium that included National City Bank and Key Bank. True to their word, both banks stepped up to the plate by strongly supporting us in front of the other banks.

At the end of that month, we reported our third quarter results. Our quarterly consolidated loss had increased to $9.2 million. But the business plans for the foreign operations had arrived on schedule. We were able to show the ten banks that we had a strategy for dealing with the crisis, and we began negotiations with them in November. We were seeking a credit line of $230 million to replace our existing line of $75 million—and we got it.

On December 4, 1992, we paid a $52.1 million bonus to our U.S. workforce. The board also approved a shareholder dividend to keep our continuous record intact. It was all borrowed money. In January, we learned that our fourth quarter consolidated loss was $19.8 million. That amount included a $7.4 million operating loss abroad and a $23.9 million restructuring charge. To put the foreign operations in a stronger position to stage a rebound, we had decided to write off unneeded and obsolete machinery and questionable inventories. Although the foreign operations had not broken into the black by year's end, we were still hopeful that the turnaround plans would work. Our loss for the whole year was $45.8 million.

In the meantime, Rolf Jonassen had resigned. He had become very wealthy when we purchased Norweld, and as the problems mounted in Europe, he apparently had had enough. In early 1993 I named Keith Cowan, the head of our Welding Technology Center, to be president of our European operations. Keith had both sales experience and the engineering skills needed to revive the manufacturing operations.

In March we signed the credit agreement with the ten banks. We thought we were over the hump. The European directors had assured us that the worst was behind them, and they seemed to be following their business plans.

But the business plans had not—and could not have—foreseen the deepening of the European recession. The plans were obliterated, and the European results for the first quarter of 1993 were again bad: an operating loss of $14.4 million. Once again, the European managers had been overly optimistic, and I had been overly trusting.

In the spring of 1993, I finally chanced to learn why the European operations had chronically missed their sales and profit targets. The operating budget of the management company in Norway was funded by the individual businesses in each country, and the size of its budget was based on the forecasted, rather than the actual, sales and profits of those businesses. To inflate the management company's own operating budget, its leaders had encouraged the businesses to submit opti-mistic—rather than realistic—forecasts. I was shocked.

In mid-May we received the numbers for April. They were devastating: Europe lost $8.2 million and the for-eign operations as a whole lost $9.6 million. We seemed certain to violate the covenants in our new credit pack-age. Once again, I had to draw on every strength in order to remain outwardly positive to our employees and board members.

A Plan to Revive the Patient

The way I saw it, we had two choices: we could resort to massive layoffs and cut executive salaries to save money, or we could make extraordinary efforts to increase revenues and profits. I never seriously considered the first option. I believed that downsizing violated everything Lincoln stood for. Our longtime covenant with our workers guaranteed them at least 30 hours of work per week.

Rather than downsize, we turned to our U.S. employees for help. Downsizing could only result in deterioration of morale, trust, and productivity. It's bad long-term business. If employees are just numbers, maybe it's easy to downsize. But when I walked into our cafeteria or onto the factory floor, I knew most of our people personally. I knew their families. I regarded Lincoln's employees as resources, not liabilities.

I also didn't buy the argument that the only obligation that responsible corporations have to their employees is to guarantee employability, not employment. We invest an enormous amount in our people and run dozens of training programs. People are trained to stay, not to be ready for dismissal.

So rather than downsize, we turned to our U.S. employees for help. I presented a 21-point plan to the board that called for our U.S. factories to boost production dramatically and for our sales force to sell our way out of the crisis. The plan called for the U.S. operation to generate a pretax, prebonus profit of $52 million, instead of the $39 million in the original budget. I also offered to move to Europe to try to minimize the hemorrhaging, once implementation of the plan was under way. The board enthusiastically endorsed the plan and my offer.

In June I went to our U.S. employees and said, "We could do what other companies have done and downsize, but we're not going to. We're going to make the U.S. company profitable enough to offset the losses abroad, remain within our bank covenants, and borrow the money again to pay the annual bonus in December. We're going to do it by increasing the top line, not by cutting back and hurting our people."

Our executives explained the company's situation and the action plan in small meetings with frontline employees. We explained the plan to our employee advisory board and circulated the minutes of the session throughout our plants. We made a video and gave people copies to take home to watch with their families. In the video, I was blunt. Management and the severe recession were to blame for the disastrous foreign expansion. "We blew it," I said. "Now we need you to bail the company out. If we violate the covenants, banks won't lend us money. And if they don't lend us money, there will be no bonus in December." That statement appealed not only to their loyalty but also to what James F. Lincoln called their "intelligent selfishness."

We then brought in our 35 district sales managers. We told them we expected them to come up with ideas and promotions that would sell the products we were gearing up to make. We also instituted a financial education program so that employees would understand that no money was being hidden from them and would see exactly how much money the U.S. operation needed to generate in order for us to be able to pay the bonus.

The all-out communication effort was critical because we needed everyone's total commitment. Rumors had created anxiety and fear on the factory floor. We needed to give people an accurate picture of the company's problems and let them know that we had a plan to fight back.

The plan called for our U.S. operation to increase sales from $1.8 million per day to $2.1 million. That was a tall order, given the still-soft U.S. economy. Some in the rank and file said, "This is foolish. We're going to gear up and by September, we'll all be on 30 hours a week." But I had faith in our sales force and knew they could sell everything we could produce. The bigger challenge would be to boost production. We were operating at 75% to 80% of capacity. The plan implied a utilization rate of more than 100%.

We got moving immediately. The factory managers were asked to eliminate every bottleneck they could possibly find. The main bottleneck, they responded, was a shortage of people. So we started hiring new employees right away.

The new people, however, needed to be trained. It can take two to three years for someone to learn how to run some of our equipment properly. It became apparent that with holidays and the traditional two-week shutdown in August, we would not have enough capacity to meet the sales targets.

That's when we started asking the veterans in the bottleneck areas to work the holidays and postpone their vacations. They came through. About 450 people in the bottleneck areas gave up 614 weeks of vacation, and some people worked seven days straight for months on end.

The employee advisory board worked closely with me and the other executives. We'd had an advisory board since 1914. It had long been a trusted means of communicating between employees and management. We used the board to apprise the workforce of our progress and maintain the momentum.

I also turned to a handful of veteran rank-and-file workers who I knew would be completely straightforward with me. I asked them to let me know when there was a potential problem—bad attitudes, bottlenecks, parts shortages. They knew how close we were to violating the covenants and that we could not afford to wait for such information to filter up through the hierarchy. We didn't have the luxury of time.

Transatlantic Culture Shock

In early June 1993 I moved to England along with my wife, Shirley, and my executive assistant, Marylee Baller. We set up a European "headquarters" in a flat in Sunningdale, an easy drive to Heathrow Airport. The U.S. operation was left in the able hands of Fred Mackenbach, a Lincoln veteran who had succeeded me as president. I didn't cut myself off totally. I received a great many faxes and phone calls each day from Fred and other managers in the United States. Fred largely ran the North American operations, while I focused on Europe and Harry Carlson, our vice chairman, dealt with the other foreign businesses.

Keith Cowan left the company shortly after I arrived in England. I had hoped to work with him, but he seemed to think my move to Europe showed a lack of confidence in him. In fact, I felt that the job was simply too much for one executive to handle alone. The crisis required someone with a stronger background in sales, and I was reluctant to transfer other executives; we needed them at home. (As a result of a virtual hiring freeze in the 1960s and 1970s, our senior ranks were now much too thin for a company of our size and complexity.) With the company on the brink of disaster and losses escalating daily, I also felt that the CEO had to be on the scene in order to make radical decisions quickly. Finally, I worried that the "barons" in the European operations would not listen to anybody but the CEO. At any rate, I was sorry to see Keith go.

As soon as I arrived in Europe, I began holding group meetings with every major sales force that handled Lincoln's products. In those meetings, every salesperson described his territory and customers and said precisely what he intended to do to get new business. It was the first time any of them had ever been required to commit themselves to a plan in front of other people.

During those months, as I met with the sales forces and managers and visited the factories, my hopes for turning around our businesses without a radical restructuring faded. Every factory was operating at 50% or less of capacity. The severity of the recession was horrifying. When I pushed managers to develop a plan for

What I saw in the German plant really alarmed me. People were not working!

increasing their market share, they told me, "The only way you increase market share is to buy another company. You never take an account from a competitor because they will retaliate and take one from you."

What I saw in the Messer plant really alarmed me. People were not working! On one visit that had been announced in advance, three "workers" were found sleeping on the job. After seeing things like that, I went to the board and said, "We have got to get out of there. We've got to close the plant no matter what the cost. It's going to sink us." We had never gotten around to trying to install the Lincoln incentive system in the plant. How naive we had been to believe that we could have.

The incentive system is transferable to some countries—especially in countries settled by immigrants, where hard work and upward mobility are ingrained parts of the culture. But in many other places, it won't easily take root. It is especially difficult to install it in a factory that has different work practices and traditions. For example, even though German factory workers are highly skilled and, in general, solid workers, they do not work nearly as hard or as long as the people in our Cleveland factory. In Germany, the average factory workweek is 35 hours. In contrast, the average workweek in Lincoln's U.S. plants is between 43 and 58 hours, and the company can ask people to work longer hours on short notice—a flexibility that is essential for the system to work. The lack of such flexibility was one reason why our approach would not work in Europe.

Happily, in September 1993 another accepted way of doing things was overturned at a trade show in Essen, Germany. Traditionally, exhibitors had used the eight-day show as a venue for entertaining customers and conducting public relations, not for making sales. There were no laws or rules against selling, but tradition prevented it. My attitude at this point was tradition be damned! To spend a couple of million dollars on a trade show and not use it to land desperately needed sales seemed absurd. I saw the show as a sales opportunity, and during our crisis we could not afford to pass up any opportunity.

We flew over three planeloads of our products from the United States and set an objective of selling 1,200 packages of semiautomatic welding equipment. We sold 1,762. By testing the conventional wisdom, we discovered that excellent American-made products *would* sell in Germany. If that was true in Germany, it undoubtedly would be true elsewhere. We could close down some of our foreign machine-manufacturing operations and still compete in foreign markets.

Changes at the Top

During my first nine months as CEO, the sheer severity and complexity of the crisis in Europe drove home the fact that the days when Lincoln could be run by one man were long gone. The company needed a bona fide management team. We needed more international expertise both in management and on the board. And we needed an independent board that would vigorously challenge the CEO. Even after my baptism by fire, I realized that I lacked in-depth international experience. I felt overwhelmed and needed help.

I had good reason to worry that if we ultimately had to take radical action overseas, our board might lack the knowledge and the stomach to do it. When the possibility of closing some of our operations was raised, several directors said, "We just bought them. Why should we close them down this soon? We should fix them, not throw them out." In my opinion, we needed new directors who did not have baggage from earlier decisions—people who would challenge long-standing assumptions and provoke or exasperate other board members, if necessary. I went to the board's nominating committee. They agreed that we needed new blood and expertise on the board and in top management.

At the May 1993 shareholders' meeting, we elected three outside directors to replace three insiders who were vice presidents of the company. The new directors were Ed Hood, retired vice chairman and executive officer of General Electric; Paul Lego, former chairman of

Westinghouse; and Larry Selhorst, CEO of American Spring Wire. A year later we brought on Henry Meyer III, president and chief operating officer of KeyCorp. All four were executives with strong international and financial experience.

We also brought in new talent at the top, even though it violated our long-standing policy of promoting from within. In 1993 Ellis Smolik retired and we recruited Jay Elliott from Goodyear as our new CFO. We were also fortunate that in 1995, Fred Stueber—an outstanding attorney at Jones, Day, Reavis & Pogue—agreed to sign on as vice president, general counsel, and secretary. It took almost a full year to find an experienced human resource executive who would fit in with Lincoln's culture, but Ray Vogt of FMC came aboard in 1996. Tony Massaro, a former Westinghouse executive with extensive international experience who had been a member of Paul Lego's team, signed on as a consultant in 1993 to help me in Europe. He did an outstanding job and consequently was named president of our European operations in January 1994. (Tony is currently chairman and CEO of all operations at Lincoln.) All four men greatly enhanced the thin management ranks.

In the fall of 1993, with the European arc-welding industry mired in excess capacity, we drew up a radical restructuring plan. We scaled down operations in the United Kingdom, Spain, France, Norway, and the Netherlands. We closed the entire Messer organization and shut down manufacturing operations in Brazil, Venezuela, and Japan. (Even though we had built the plant in Japan—going so far as to have the property blessed in a Shinto ceremony—virtually no one would buy our products, mainly because we had "insulted" the

Japanese by not having a Japanese partner.) Our restructuring charge for the year was $70.1 million.

Turning It Around

Fortunately, there was plenty of good news from the United States. Under the dynamic leadership of John Stropki, who was then our general sales manager, we not only achieved the $2.1-million-a-day sales target, we even surpassed it. (John is currently president of North American operations.) By the end of 1993, daily sales had climbed to $3.1 million, and they would stay at that level throughout 1994 and beyond. We didn't miss a beat in production. Our workers are still proud of this accomplishment, and they should be.

Of course, many others played a big part. Our engineers came out with new products, such as a line for the light commercial and home market segments that we sold through Home Depot and Wal-Mart. And we offered special promotions to our longtime distributors that proved highly successful.

Lincoln also benefited from public interest in the company's incentive system and its 40-year record of no layoffs. Dick Sabo, director of public relations, parlayed this interest into a series of television specials, including a favorable *60 Minutes* segment. Such recognition introduced Lincoln's products to the general public and helped raise the top line.

We also had some luck. Just as we were beginning to boost our production, the market started to revive—although nobody in the industry felt it yet. As a result, the upturn caught our competitors by surprise; they were still cutting back. We were already cranked up and in a position to take market share, even with the price increases that we felt were necessary. Raising prices at the time was a calculated risk, but our highly trained sales force made the new prices stick. By October 1993 it was clear that Lincoln would be okay.

Thanks to the Herculean effort in the factories and in the field, we were able to increase revenues and profits enough in the United States to avoid violating our loan covenants. The remarkable performance of the company's U.S. workers put us in a solid position to ask the banks for new covenants in November. They approved them only two days before we were scheduled to pay the bonus. On December 4, 1993, we paid a gross bonus of $55.3 million with borrowed money. Including the restructuring charge, we lost $38.1 million that year.

In the first half of 1994, we negotiated and carried out the plant closings. By mid-1994, the European and other foreign operations were in the black. Our new export strategy—which included selling American-made machines worldwide and rethinking which of our plants around the world could best serve a given market—was a smashing success. Moreover, in countries where we had closed operations, market share actually increased.

We also began rebuilding our balance sheet in 1994. I went to our U.S. workers in July and carefully explained that we were going to begin investing in the future again. The priorities were reducing our debt and increasing capital expenditures, which had been slashed during the crisis. Accordingly, we would have to reduce the individual bonuses paid that year. With prosperity returning, our people were understanding of the need to reduce the debt. In December we again paid a collective bonus of over $55 million: we didn't cut the total amount, but because of all the new hires, it was spread among more workers.

We had had a better year all the way through. Our goals for the year were for our consolidated operations to achieve the highest sales, earnings per share, and return on investment in the history of our company—and we met them. We expanded our customer base and introduced new high-tech products. After the bonus payout, we earned $48.0 million for the year, a one-year turnaround of almost $86 million. At the end of 1994, my wife, my assistant, and I moved back to Ohio. The crisis was over.

Harsh Lessons Learned

The root cause of the crisis was that Lincoln's leaders, including myself, had grown overconfident in the company's abilities and systems. We had long boasted that our unique culture and incentive system—along with the dedicated, skilled workforce that the company had built over the decades—were the main source of Lincoln's competitive advantage. We had assumed that the incentive system and culture could be transferred abroad and that the workforce could be quickly replicated. We had scoffed at all the faddists in the business world who were jumping on the empowerment bandwagon, smugly noting that teamwork and open communication had long been a way of life at Lincoln. Yet we had ignored the loud and widespread expressions of concern from employees who saw our foreign expansion as a highly risky adventure. We had been naive to think that we could instantly become a global company with Lincoln's limited management resources. Although we went through a couple of nightmare years, we did finally learn from our mistakes.

Competing globally requires a lot more time, money, and management resources than we realized. At least five years before we launched our expansion program in 1987, we should have started building a management team and a board of directors from whom we could have learned how to proceed. We also should have allocated at least twice the money that we budgeted and assumed that we would suffer some setbacks. Instead, we jumped headfirst into a hornet's nest, confident that our manufacturing technology and incentive system would pull us through.

The company is now much more careful about foreign acquisitions. It will build a new plant but only with a partner in a joint venture. Recently, it has purchased a wire company in Canada, entered a joint venture in Turkey, and formed alliances in the emerging markets of Indonesia, Malaysia, and China.

The only new place where Lincoln has successfully transplanted the incentive system is in Mexico City. That may sound surprising because the plant, which we bought in 1990, was unionized, and piecework runs against the Mexican culture. But we introduced the system gradually. The plant had about 175 workers, and we began by asking two of them to take a chance on piecework. We also put a net under them—that is, we guaranteed them a minimum income. After they started making more money than their counterparts, people started asking if they could go onto the system, too. It took about two years, but the entire operation eventually adopted piecework. If it is done slowly and properly, the system can be introduced into some existing organizations or cultures where it might not seem to fit.

Since 1994 the company has continued to prosper; each year has brought increased market share along with record sales and earnings. The balance sheet is strong again. In 1995 revenues topped $1 billion, we had a successful public offering, and the debt-to-equity ratio dropped from its one-time high of 63% to less than 12%. Lincoln's shareholders saw the company's value almost double from 1994 through 1998. The company continues to generate cash and recently announced a stock buyback program to further strengthen the balance sheet and improve shareholder value.

Lincoln now has an internationally experienced board of directors and management team and is a lot wiser thanks to the harsh lessons of the past. Having largely regained the trust of its people, the company can continue to move into the tumultuous realm of globalization, with a clear-eyed view of both the pitfalls and the opportunities.

Originally published in May–June 1999
Reprint 99305

About the Contributors

Prior to his retirement in 1997, NORMAN R. AUGUSTINE served as Chairman and CEO of Martin Marietta, and subsequently Lockheed Martin Corporation, for a total of approximately ten years. Since that time, he has served on the faculty of the School of Engineering and Applied Science at Princeton University. Earlier in his career, he held a number of positions in the Pentagon, including Undersecretary of the Army. He has served as President of the Boy Scouts of America and is currently in his eighth year as Chairman of the Red Cross. He serves on the boards of Lockheed Martin, Philips Petroleum, Procter & Gamble, and Black & Decker. His most recent management book is *Shakespeare in Charge*, written in collaboration with Kenneth Adelman.

GREG BRENNEMAN is President, COO, and board member of Continental Airlines. Brenneman, along with Continental's Chairman and CEO, Gordon Bethune, pioneered one of the most remarkable turnarounds in corporate America by focusing on reengineering key areas of the airline, including scheduling, pricing, maintenance, reservations, customer service, and employee relations. He holds an MBA from Harvard Business School and a BA of Business in Accounting and Finance from Washburn University.

DONALD F. HASTINGS is the Chairman Emeritus for The Lincoln Electric Company. During his career of 44 years at

Lincoln, he worked as a Salesman, District Sales Manager, General Sales Manager, Vice President of Sales, President, Chairman, and CEO. He was also Chairman of the Board of Governors of the National Electric Manufacturers Association (NEMA), Chairman of Cleveland World Trade Center, and is currently Chairman and CEO of the Cleveland Council on World Affairs.

LINDA HILL is the Wallace Brett Donham Professor of Business Administration in the Department of Organizational Behavior at Harvard Business School. Her consulting and executive education activities have been in the areas of managing change, managing interfunctional relationships, career management, and career development. She is the author of *Becoming a Manager, Power and Influence*, and two NewMedia Invision award-winning multimedia management development programs on CD-ROM: *High Performance Management* and *Coaching*. She is currently a member of the Board of Directors of Cooper Industries, the Board of Trustees of the Rockefeller Foundation, Bryn Mawr College, and The Children's Museum of Boston, and the Board of Overseers of the Beth Israel Deaconess Medical Center, Boston.

IDALENE F. KESNER is the Frank P. Popoff Professor of Strategic Management at Indiana University's Kelley School of Business. She is also Director of the school's Consulting Academy and teaches in the areas of strategic management, crisis management, change management, and management consulting. She has taught in over 60 different executive education programs, and she has served as a consultant for many different national and international firms. Her research interests focus on corporate boards of directors, chief executive succession, corporate governance, and mergers and acquisitions. She currently serves on the board of directors for two U.S. firms and one Canadian firm.

JOHN A. QUELCH is Dean of London Business School and a Professor at London University. He was formerly the S.S. Kresge Professor of Marketing at Harvard Business School. An expert on consumer goods and global marketing, he sits on the boards of four public companies in the United States and the United Kingdom.

ANURAG SHARMA is an Associate Professor at the Eugene M. Isenberg School of Management, University of Massachusetts at Amherst. His research has been published in several publications, including *California Management Review*, *Strategic Management Journal*, *Academy of Management Journal*, and *Academy of Management Review*. He writes and consults in the areas of business strategy and corporate innovation.

N. CRAIG SMITH is Associate Professor at the McDonough School of Business at Georgetown University, and Visiting Professor of Marketing at INSEAD. He specializes in marketing management with a focus on business ethics, and consults with firms on problems in this area. His current research projects examine product recalls, ethical decision-making in marketing, ethical issues in marketing research, consumer boycotts, and corporate citizenship. He is the author of three books, *Ethics in Marketing*, *The Management Research Handbook*, and *Morality and the Market*, and has published articles in journals such as *Harvard Business Review*, *Sloan Management Review*, *Journal of Marketing*, and *Journal of Retailing*.

Journalist and fiction writer **SANDI SONNENFELD** is a graduate of Mount Holyoke College and holds an MFA in Creative Writing from the University of Washington. Her work has appeared in a wide variety of publications including *Harvard Business Review*, *Wall Street Journal*'s *National Business Employment Weekly*, *Media Inc.*, and *The Employment Paper* in Seattle. She is currently Senior Account Executive with Publicis Dialog, ranked among the top 30 public relations firms in the nation.

ROBERT J. THOMAS is Professor at the McDonough School of Business at Georgetown University. He specializes in new product development and marketing strategy. His research interests include topics in new product design, market segmentation, forecasting, and the management of innovation. He has authored several articles and books, including his most recent book, *New Product Success Stories.* He is on the editorial board of the *Journal of Product Innovation Management* and has provided expert testimony on demand for the Federal Communications Commission, the U.S. Postal Rate Commission, and the International Trade Commission.

SUZY WETLAUFER, formerly of the international management consulting firm Bain & Company, is a Senior Editor of the *Harvard Business Review*, specializing in the area of leadership, teams, and organizational psychodynamics. In addition to "After the Layoffs, What Next?" and "Leadership When There is No One to Ask," she is the author or coauthor of numerous *HBR* pieces including "What's Killing the Creativity at Coolburst?" and "A Question of Color."

Note: *Information provided within each article about the contributors to case studies was applicable at the time of original publication.*

Index